"If you are that conscientious teacher who sees it as part of their mi... understand what is happening to students in transition, D. M. Maynard's workbook focusing on trans and non-binary students will take you on a deeply self-reflective journey that embraces the true calling of a teacher. During a time where the paths of gender identity and schools are crossing, this book is designed to help teachers, staff, and schools understand the school experience through the lens of TGNB students, and the crucial role teachers have in providing a safe and positive social and emotional environment that all children deserve."

Lorenzo Licopoli, Ph.D., Interim Superintendent of Schools of Arlington Central School District, Retired Superintendent of Schools, Board Trustee for Northport USFD, and Educational Consultant

"This timely and relevant workbook provides a comprehensive framework for all educators and support staff who want to empower themselves with the knowledge, tools, and confidence to support transgender, non-binary, and gender non-conforming students. This detailed workbook allows the reader to move at their own pace, work alone or with a team, and take a deep dive into the unique needs of TGNB and/or gender questioning students. A must have resource for educators who want to create an affirming school environment for all students."

Kimberly Hession, LCSWR, HS School Social Worker on Long Island, NY, Co-Owner of Great South Bay Therapy, and Co-Founder of Coastal Practice Consultants, LLC

"D. M. Maynard's workbook is exactly the resource which has been missing that teaches educators practical methods on how to support the transgender and non-binary student population. This book enables us to understand and assist our TGNB students during their transition. The author truly captures ways all school personnel can help TGNB students navigate school life while in transition. Definitely a must read for educators!"

Ashley Barros, MS, TESOL Certified, Fifth Grade Special Education Teacher for DOE, Brooklyn, NY

"Finally, there is a tool which sheds light on appropriate ways teachers, support staff, and administrators can advocate for TGNB students in school. D. M. Maynard has crafted a book that addresses the many questions educators need answered to support the gender transition of their students. No school professional's library is complete without this esteemed workbook!"

Ida D. Ayres, SAS/SDA, Retired Principal, Co-Author of The Elementary School Principal's Calendar: A Month-by-Month Planner for the School Year, Former: Director of Placement at Molloy College and Adjunct Professor, St. John's University

"As a teacher I highly recommend that all educators purchase this workbook for it addresses the needs of students who are transitioning and how a school environment should be to ensure that the modern classroom is a safe place for all students. D. M. Maynard creates a well-informed, well-researched workbook with exercises that require self-reflection for all educators and staff. This book should be the focus of professional development all around the country in these times of much change within society and education."

Robert DiBella, M.Ed., HS Social Studies Teacher for New York City Public Schools, Bronx, NY and Author/Screenwriter

"Maynard's incredible workbook offers insight that shines a light of clarity into the needs of TGNB students for school personnel in a way that is approachable and relatable. As someone who has spent over 30 years in the educational field, I am inspired by D. M.'s clear approach to some very complex understandings—an amazing resource for everyone!"

Dan Phillips, MS, CCC-SLP, Educational Technology Specialist, Founder/Creator and Current Director of the Technology Resource Center of Marin, and CEO/Founder of the Nika Project

"The reflective nature of this vital and necessary resource will increase school personnel's understanding of TGNB students' experiences and needs as they transition. It presents educators with the opportunity to think deeply about their own beliefs and feelings, and how these views affect their support of students. D. M. Maynard's workbook provides teachers, support staff, and administrators with specific strategies that will have a positive impact on staff and students. Every administrator should buy a copy of the book for each of their school buildings!"

Sheryl Goffman, M.Ed., Assistant Superintendent for Curriculum, Instruction, and Assessment, Rye City School District, NY, Former: Deputy Superintendent, Director of Elementary Education, Elementary Principal, Special Education Teacher, Educational Consultant, and Adjunct Professor

"D. M. Maynard has done it again! Her new workbook is designed to guide and teach educators about TGNB students and provides insight into the complexity of a TGNB student's world. As always Maynard's knowledge and passion are evident on every page. Every child deserves to be educated in a safe and caring environment and this workbook helps make that a reality for TGNB students."

Michael P. Nagler, Ed.D., Superintendent of Mineola Public Schools, 2020 NYS Superintendent of the Year, and 2020 National Superintendent Finalist

"This reflective workbook gently invites educators, who may be stepping into uncharted or uncomfortable territory, to do the work it takes to understand and support students who are transgender and non-binary. D. M. Maynard's experience, compassion, and expertise guide and inspire the reader to take action. This essential resource is an important component in ensuring ALL students are seen, respected, and valued."

Gary Wellbrock, Ph.D., First Grade Teacher at The American Sign Language and English Lower School in NYC, Adjunct Professor at Fordham University, and Founder of Broadway Books First Class

"Should you want to get it right, you need to read this book! The material in this workbook can be life-saving for TGNB youth. Misinformation or lack of information can cause a well-intended educator to cause trauma and long-term harm during a child's transformative years. It is quite evident that D. M. Maynard has worked countless hours to make sure this book is thorough and yet simple enough for anyone to understand and actually enjoy using it."

Emma Luz Stovall, BSW, proud parent of a transgender teen, parent advocate for the Ackerman Institute's Gender and Family Project, served in the ARMY Reserves, and is a Law Enforcement Officer with the NYC Department of Probation

"Kudos to D. M. Maynard for writing this innovative and timely workbook to assist teachers, support staff, and administrators in creating schools where all transgender nonbinary (TGNB) students and/or those who are questioning their gender feel safe, included, and respected every day. As a pediatrician, adolescent medicine sub specialist, and medical director for seven school-based health centers serving 23 public schools in NYC, I am keenly aware of what a marvelous and much needed resource this is for educators striving to provide the support every student needs so they can reach their educational potential and make a difference in every child's life. Take the time to read and work through the workbook's exercises …and watch yourself grow!"

Melanie A. Gold, DO, DMQ (she/her/hers), Professor of Pediatrics and Population & Family Health, Columbia University Irving Medical Center and Medical Director of School-Based Health Centers, New York-Presbyterian Hospital

THE REFLECTIVE WORKBOOK FOR TEACHERS AND SUPPORT STAFF OF TRANS AND NON-BINARY STUDENTS

by the same author

The Reflective Workbook for Parents and Families of Transgender and Non-Binary Children
Your Transition as Your Child Transitions
D. M. Maynard
ISBN 978 1 78775 236 8
eISBN 978 1 78775 237 5

The Reflective Workbook for Partners of Transgender People
Your Transition as Your Partner Transitions
D. M. Maynard
ISBN 978 1 78592 772 0
eISBN 978 1 78450 672 8

of related interest

The Educator's Guide to LGBT+ Inclusion
A Practical Resource for K-12 Teachers, Administrators, and School Support Staff
Kryss Shane, MS, MSW, LSW, LMSW
Foreword by PostSecret. Afterword by James Lecesne
ISBN 978 1 78775 108 8
eISBN 978 1 78775 109 5

Supporting Gender Diversity in Early Childhood Classrooms
A Practical Guide
*Encian Pastel, Katie Steele, Julie Nicholson, Cyndi Maurer, Julia
Hennock, Jonathan Julian, Tess Unger and Nathanael Flynn*
ISBN 978 1 78592 819 2
eISBN 978 1 78450 914 9

THE REFLECTIVE WORKBOOK

FOR **TEACHERS** AND **SUPPORT STAFF** OF **TRANS** AND **NON-BINARY STUDENTS**

Your School's Transition as
Your Students Transition

D. M. Maynard

Jessica Kingsley Publishers
London and Philadelphia

First published in Great Britain in 2021 by Jessica Kingsley Publishers
An Hachette Company

1

Copyright © D. M. Maynard 2021

A CIP catalogue record for this title is available from the British Library and the Library of Congress

ISBN 978 1 78775 217 7
eISBN 978 1 78775 218 4

Printed and bound in the United States by Integrated Books International

Jessica Kingsley Publishers' policy is to use papers that are natural, renewable and recyclable products and made from wood grown in sustainable forests. The logging and manufacturing processes are expected to conform to the environmental regulations of the country of origin.

Jessica Kingsley Publishers
Carmelite House
50 Victoria Embankment
London EC4Y 0DZ

www.jkp.com

This workbook is dedicated to you, the teachers and support staff,
who entered this profession to make a positive difference and serve as role models
by committing to support and being willing to learn how to help and
protect your students throughout their gender journey,
for your voices matter and must be heard
as you advocate for the human rights and respect every student deserves!

CONTENTS

ACKNOWLEDGMENTS

First and foremost, I want to express my gratitude to all of my former students—Thank you for teaching me more than I ever taught you, for helping me grow alongside you, and for more than 30 years of experiencing absolute joy in your presence. It has been both my honor and privilege to have been any part of your precious lives...the gifts you all gave me are forever imprinted in my heart!

To Susan Leftoff Barash (my fourth grade teacher) and Linda Restaino-Merola (my junior high school reading teacher)—Thank you for teaching me to read so that years later I could do the same for others, for never giving up on me, and for creating the most enduring blueprints I still follow as an educator...I credit you both with the bulk of my success, for without your influence on my life, I would not have had the career opportunities I experienced and enjoyed in the past and continue to have today.

To Ida Ayres—Thank you for recognizing my potential from that first 45-minute, student teacher interview and then changing the trajectory of my life. You were my first mentor and the one who offered me a chance of a lifetime. I will always be eternally grateful to you for enabling me to follow my greatest passion!

To Sherri Goffman—Thank you for serving as an educational role model, constantly raising me up in every way, celebrating all aspects of who I am, and always putting children first!

To Larry "Prince Charming" Licopoli—Thank you for encouraging me to be myself as you kindly cheered me on as I did so, repeatedly opening so many pathways to help me shine, collaboratively joining me on many a venture, and supporting all the roads I traveled.

To Mike Nagler—Thank you for instilling in me the importance of questioning in all its forms, showing me the power of thinking outside of the box, ever reminding me to focus more on the process than the product, leading me to understand all that is possible, and protecting me when I was most vulnerable.

To my supportive cheerleaders—Marlene Aryan, Barbara Baughan, Sam Eber, Hakan Eber, Michael George, Nicklas Hållén, Judie Halpern, Denise Lasiuk, Sofie Lasiuk, Mary Marino, Gail Moskowitz, Martha Murphy-George, Bill O'Brien, Maureen O'Brien, Solomon Shapiro, Dr. Richard Shear, and Jonathan Sutton: Thank you all for your sincere reassurance and belief in my abilities.

To Mom, Dad, Aunt Sue, Uncle Steve, and my sister Stacy—As always, I write with all of you as the angels on my shoulders.

To Mia and Andreia—Thank you for being pioneers, wise beyond your years, and my courageous teachers.

To the Jessica Kingsley Publishers Team—Thank you for this glorious opportunity, for all of your creative talents, and for making yet another lifelong dream of mine come true.

To Andrew James, my incredible and supportive Editorial Director—Thank you for always making yourself available to talk with me, for guiding me with infinite respect, and for your constant cooperative spirit...you are fantastic in every way and then some!

To Emily Badger, Katelynn Bartleson, Yojaira Cordero, David Corey, Giuliana di Mitrio, Alicia Friele, Kath Mackrill, Isabel Martin, Adam Peacock, Victoria Peters, Colin Wood, Julia Zullo, and most especially Emma Holak, my Bonus Team at JKP—Thank you for your splendid professionalism, valuable touches, and clear zeal for publishing.

To Christie Block, MA, MS, CCC-SLP, David Bradlee, DO, S.J. Langer, LCSWR, Jonathan Lyons, Kristen Molloy, Katherine Rachlin, PhD, and Chris Straayer—Thank you for generously extending your specialized knowledge to me when I needed it most.

To Stephen Terzuoli, Frances Vella, and Wendy Yalowitz—Thank you for listening with your heart and for sustaining me as I completed this workbook.

To Simon Langer—Thank you for offering your exceptional skills as you captured my essence through the lens of your camera with your gifted and artistic abilities.

To Hakan Eber—Thank you for improving what was in-"over"stock, polishing it well, and releasing its radiance!

To my LG Friends: Amaya, Aya, Christel, Ghita, Hani, Khalil, Maryse, Reine, Yara, and Yoanna—Thank you for expanding my world, brightening my days, and always welcoming me with open arms...I am better for knowing all of you!

To my chapter editors—Rosemary Capelle, Teresa Dawber, Nancy "My G!" Ekloff, Mary LoCascio, Cheryl Minsky, Donna Restivo, Benay Shear, and Dee Wojis: Thank you for being the most dedicated and caring teachers and support staff that I have ever known, for I am proud to call you my friends and to have worked among you for decades as you encouragingly shaped the minds and hearts of every child who has entered your classrooms and/or offices year after year. I greatly appreciate the precious time and honorable manner in which you offered important editing suggestions!

To Maria "Only You!" Riccardi—Thank you for being my classroom partner for more than a decade, for keeping up with me and my piles, for always saying YES to everything, for laughing with me for hours on end, and for continuously being someone I can count on in and out of school.

To my "Late Night" editor, 24/7 shoulder to lean on, and cherished "HEELLLOOOO" friend — Pat Molloy: Thank you beyond words for carrying me across the finish line once more, offering me your extensive-educational expertise and treasured advice, endless time, intellectual "honorific" insight, faith in yet another project, and abundance of assistance throughout the entire process of writing this workbook. Your tenacious input truly made the difference and I am eternally grateful to you, my Sista!

To my husband Simon—Thank you for continuously believing in my ideas, helping me through the sleepless nights, being a power of example in more ways than I could ever express loudly enough, and choosing me to be your life partner…I love you unconditionally and know that you have been instrumental in making this journey possible while most significantly, you have been by my side and lifted me to the highest of heights. Always remember, wherever you are, that is where I wish to call home!

Chapter 1

YOUR PRIVATE SPACE: AN INTRODUCTION

It takes a special type of calling to become a teacher or school administrator. With this privilege comes great responsibility. Teachers not only provide the essential knowledge vital for the academic growth of students, but also are often required to fulfill the roles of parents, therapists, medical assistants, and social mentors to students six to eight hours a day. In addition, support staff enhance, enrich, and ensure further expertise needed to guarantee a student's progress. Teachers and support staff work together to build a strong foundation that is critical for student achievement. Moreover, school administrators create, shape, and promote the policies and procedures that enable teachers and support staff to successfully fulfill their various responsibilities. In fact, in most cases, students spend more of their waking hours under the care of those who work in their schools than in the presence of their parents. For these reasons and more, it is crucial that while attending school, all students feel nurtured, respected, and honored by school personnel.

I often think of the teacher who most impacted my learning and influenced the philosophy that guided my entire teaching career. Identifying that a large number of us in my fourth grade class struggled with being able to read on grade level, she accepted us for who we were as learners and instinctually understood the methods she needed to implement in order for us to accomplish reading on level. She made the conscious decision to allow us to read any form of reading materials, as long as we read and improved our skills. I recall the classroom being filled with cartoon strips, scripts from a variety of plays, poetry, comic books, lyrics from famous Broadway songs, and magazines. She intuitively knew that we could not relate to the stories in traditional basal readers. By the end of the year, we all soared academically and I knew she had positively affected the trajectory of our lives forever.

During my more than 30-year tenure as a teacher, I recognized that gender non-conforming students were present in my classroom. Realizing this, I intentionally fostered an environment that embraced their gender diversity and innate expressive preferences without judgment or a desire to change them in any way. Akin to my elementary school teacher, I made it my mission to nurture all of them and celebrate the style in which every student displayed their gender expression. Many of these students' parents had privately shared both their gratitude and concerns. Instead of shying away from any controversy, I used differences of opinion as opportunities to lead by example and share my practices with any colleague who would listen. When met with opposition, I made the conscious decision to continuously reevaluate how I would approach these professional obstacles and move forward.

After educating young minds for more than 20 years, I was teaching a student who was assigned male at birth and from the very beginning of the year this student much preferred the company of their female classmates. In addition, whenever this child chose to play in any centers or with toys, they elected to pick those that were typically associated with females in Western culture. Moreover, this student's absolute treasure was a sparkly tutu that was in the family center. Most days this child pulled the skirt over their head, then down to their neck area, eventually flipped it over, and called it their hair. This student would often request to wear it like this all day long until dismissal time. Since it did not interfere with the student's learning or anyone else's, it never became an issue in my classroom. I had witnessed these kinds of actions in varying ways and degrees for more than two decades. I began to understand that this behavior may be common for students who are given the freedom to choose items or activities according to their likes and interests. It is important to realize that this does not necessarily mean a student is questioning their gender or will ever identify on the transgender spectrum.

Nevertheless, for some students, these choices could be the beginning or a continuation of behaviors that will align with how a child truly identifies when living in their affirmed gender. Approximately three months after this particular child was in my class, all students were instructed to draw a self-portrait for a required assessment that would later be shown to their parents. As part of the evaluation, students were encouraged to dictate a sentence or two to describe themselves. As I was transcribing for this student and asked who the person was in this drawing, they proudly stated, "Me!" The picture was of a child wearing a dress, with long hair, and sporting the biggest smile. A week later, I met alone with one of this student's parents for a conference and showed them the self-portrait. The parent did not appear surprised. We had a very lengthy conversation in which the parent bravely shared a phone video of their child living in their affirmed gender at home. After viewing the video, this parent and I began a journey of understanding and learning that changed the course of my teaching and more importantly, this child and their family's life forever. Though I had been quite experienced with the wishes of gender-diverse students, I was not as knowledgeable about the needs of transgender and non-binary (TGNB) students. I knew I had an obligation to educate myself in order to be of service to all TGNB students who would enter the grounds of my school in the future. I promised myself on the day of observing the video, from that moment forward, I would dedicate my professional career to helping those working in schools become knowledgeable in how to support TGNB students and improve their school experience.

As a result, many of my colleagues and other educators became more and more aware that I was presenting workshops at conferences to teach educators how to incorporate practices and policies that honored the school lives of TGNB students. Many faculty members and other professionals I knew outside my school began to ask me questions about the TGNB students who were in their classrooms and schools. Their questions were candid but kind and the teachers were genuinely hungry for knowledge, while letting me know they did not know who else to ask. For months on end, they would bring thoughtful questions and share scenarios with me, hoping I could shed some light on their confusion and assist them in supporting their TGNB students. That is when the lightbulb went off in my head and the concept for this workbook was born!

All school employees need to understand that schools have always had students who identify on the transgender spectrum. As these youths' rights and voices bravely come to the forefront, school personnel must learn ways to keep them safe, included, and respected on a daily basis. TGNB students and/or those questioning their gender should never be silenced, bullied, or ignored. It is not enough if some laws state that these students be treated properly. It is the duty of every teacher, support staff, and administrator to recognize the critical role they can play in the safety, education, and well-being of these students. With this realization, it is crucial for schools to remain current and change with the times.

It can be very challenging for educators to be given a directive that is in contrast to their personal beliefs or educational philosophies. I have always been a strong-willed and outspoken educator who has expressed what I thought was best for my students and school. Moreover, I was able to implement what was requested of me after researching the facts and posing critical questions with the end goal of gaining the information I needed to proceed. Many educators, like myself, believe we work for the students and that their family members are an extension of them. Therefore, we have an obligation to abide by what they all feel is best for the student in accordance with laws and school policies. Some teachers have shared with me that when they were faced with an option to which they were personally resistant, they found it helpful to put themselves in the shoes of the student or family member who was making the appeal. The question they asked themselves was, "How would I want teachers, support staff, and other school personnel to respond if I were asking for something vital for my child or family member?" Once it was framed in this manner, honoring what was mandated in respect to the needs of TGNB students became automatic and acceptable for most educators, even for those who were originally uncomfortable with doing so.

There is no doubt that there may be teachers, support staff, and administrators who will refuse to accept these students. However, there are many who will easily embrace those on the transgender spectrum but honestly do not know where or how to begin the process of addressing all that is necessary within the school environment and its changing culture. This resource enables educators to examine past beliefs and teachings. It offers a safe space for self-reflection, realistic practices, and consideration of the experiences of others to empower educators to successfully work with TGNB students within their classrooms and in school. It will all be approached without judgment, malice, or blame. This workbook will also afford a place for teachers, support staff, and administrators to silently voice and journal their concerns, untangle misinformation, discover the unknowns, and learn about themselves while becoming leaders in relation to trans issues. This vital resource is highly recommended for *all* school personnel, regardless of their current views and level of acceptance, as their school navigates welcoming and supporting those students who are questioning their gender and/or who may identify on the transgender spectrum.

Thus, this unique workbook contains the dos and don'ts, self-reflective questions, and easy-to-use exercises that I designed to help me discover and understand how to support TGNB students. By incorporating graphic organizers, responsive techniques, interactive games, and Sampler Shares, this book enables teachers and support staff to utilize familiar tools that enhance instructional practices.

This book focuses on guiding all school personnel to acquire and process important information that will help them fulfill the needs of TGNB and/or gender questioning students attending their schools. Instead of offering a set curriculum, this publication provides an opportunity for all to explore their own concerns and unmask their possible biases. Educators will learn how to implement communication exercises and increase the understanding they seek through a myriad of activities that enable teachers, support staff, and school administrators to view trans matters through the lens of their TGNB and/or gender questioning students. Moreover, this workbook will focus on gender, not sexuality. Many books that state they are LGBTQ+ (lesbian, gay, bisexual, transgender, queer or questioning, plus others) centered, focus more on "LGB" and sometimes "Q" related information, rather than on "T" topics. As a result, trans issues can become overlooked or not given their proper and necessary platform. This is not the case for this book. Though some students may be questioning or defining their gender and sexuality at the same time, the emphasis will primarily be on gender, in all of its forms, and the ways gender identity impacts the daily lives of TGNB and/or gender questioning students.

Knowing that all those who work in school settings are constantly required to add more and more to their insurmountable workload and are pulled in every direction in order to be equitable to the needs of all students, I felt it was imperative that I provided a user-friendly resource that was relevant to their teaching. As an educator, I knew it was important that the suggestions were easy to implement, while meeting professionals where they were in relation to the topic. Rarely is there a resource that assists all school personnel in ways that enhance their own journey as they navigate and experience working with students who are on the transgender spectrum and/or are questioning their gender. This workbook is intentionally written for teachers, support staff, and school administrators who are yearning to be appropriately prepared and knowledgeable in order to validate and nurture the TGNB and/or gender questioning students in their school, but do not have the guidance or tools yet. As Trans Studies and Trans communities come to the forefront of society, so do the challenges and experiences of teachers, support staff, and school administrators who are personally responsible for assisting and guiding different aspects of the lives of TGNB and/or gender questioning students. This resource is the answer for all educators and school personnel who truly have a desire to understand, support, and accept the TGNB and/or gender questioning students in their school.

AUTHOR'S DISCLAIMER NOTES

- Whenever the words *teacher, teachers,* and *support staff* are used, they will be the umbrella term for and will also refer to: administrators, community members, school personnel, board members, and educators.

- The word *trans* will be used throughout the workbook and will serve as the umbrella term to include every and all gender identities and gender expressions a student feels aligns with their affirmed gender that may be different from their gender assigned at birth.

- It should be noted that each student must be referred to and about in the manner in which they identify themselves. Though, for some, the way one individual identifies may be found unacceptable or offensive by another, every person must be asked how they identify, as well as their affirmed name and pronoun/s, and this response must be honored.

- The inclusive use of the word *trans* is embedded within and will incorporate (but is not limited to) these words and terms: transgender, trans-identified, in transition, non-binary, gender non-binary, questioning, gender questioning, questioning their gender, genderqueer, gender fluid, gender diverse, gender expansive, gender creative, gender non-conforming, intersex, transgender/gender diverse (TGD), transgender and gender non-binary (TGNB), transgender non-conforming (TGNC), and identifying on the transgender spectrum. It should be noted that children and adults may hold more than one of these identities at the same time, for a certain time period, or over their lifetime.

- These terms will be interchangeable and understood as inclusive of (but are not limited to) any of the possible singular and multiple ways a student may identify; therefore, whenever the word *student* is used, it refers to any student who identifies themselves as: transgender, trans-identified, in transition, non-binary, gender non-binary, questioning, gender questioning, questioning their gender, genderqueer, gender fluid, gender diverse, gender expansive, gender creative, gender non-conforming, intersex, TGD, TGNB, TGNC, and identifying on the transgender spectrum.

- The words and terms *transition, the transition, in transition, transition process,* and *transitioning* shall be used throughout the workbook and will be both interchangeable with and refer to (but are not limited to) the words and terms: gender questioning, questioning their gender; and may also be part of the gender-affirming process for those students and children who identify as transgender, trans-identified, in transition, non-binary, gender non-binary, questioning, gender questioning, questioning their gender, genderqueer, gender fluid, gender diverse, gender expansive, gender creative, gender non-conforming, intersex, TGD, TGNB, TGNC, and identifying on the transgender spectrum.

- In reference to pronouns: *they/them/their* will often be used as a singular pronoun throughout the workbook, as well as *he/him/his* and *she/her/hers.*

- All TGNB and/or gender questioning individuals referred to in this workbook will always be referred to by their affirmed gender, even when referring to them in the past, unless they have requested this should not occur. In some cases, the pronouns of *they/their/them* will be used as the gender-neutral pronoun to refer to an individual if their gender must be kept anonymous or they have not indicated a pronoun preference.

- For the purposes of this book, when sexuality is mentioned, it is specifically referring to sexual orientation.

- Important information that students, teachers, support staff, administrators, board members, school personnel, and community members need to know: for some children and adults, the transition process continues throughout their lifetime; for others, the transition is considered over once all the social and/or medical interventions desired are completed.

- When speaking with parents and other family members, it is important to understand specific ways the transition process can be viewed. For some parents and family members, the duration of the transition process of the child can be connected to one of the two circumstances stated above or based on the period when the major focus of their time is concentrated on the transition, in its varied forms. Many parents I know or who have attended my workshops refer to their relationship with their child in terms of before, during, and after the transition or the time it took to navigate their child's affirmed gender, referring to *after* for the period when the topic of the transition is no longer front and center on a daily basis. This disclaimer is included to acknowledge and honor those for whom the transitioning period is never over, for whom the word *after* may never apply.

- When the term *family members* is used, it refers to the members of a single family; however, when the word *families* is used, it refers to multiple families.

- It is important to recognize that whenever the term *parent* is used, it will also be the umbrella term for and refer to: guardians and caregivers.

- It is recognized that more than one person in a family can identify as (but not be limited to): transgender, trans-identified, in transition, non-binary, gender non-binary, questioning, gender questioning, questioning their gender, genderqueer, gender fluid, gender diverse, gender expansive, gender creative, gender non-conforming, intersex, TGD, TGNB, TGNC, and on the transgender spectrum.

- The workbook is offered to give voice from the perspective of teachers, support staff, and anyone else who interacts with a student in and out of a school setting who is affirming and/or questioning their gender. This workbook is intended to help anyone who is searching for a reflective resource in regard to any aspect of their students' social and/or medical transition as they are identifying on the transgender spectrum, are in transition, have transitioned, are questioning their gender, identifying as non-binary, or are living in their affirmed gender.

- In reference to the stage your student may be at this moment, this workbook is intended to be useful for those teachers, support staff, and anyone else who interacts with a student in and out of a school setting who is beginning any aspect of the transition process, is questioning their gender, or is discovering what they need to feel whole in relation to their affirmed gender. The focus of most of the vignettes, questions, tools, and exercises contained within this workbook is for teachers, support staff, and anyone else who interacts with a student in and out of a school setting if and when they consider transitioning or are in the transition process.

· The phrase *TGNB and/or gender questioning students* is used in this book; however, for portions of this workbook *and/or gender questioning* may not follow the term *TGNB students*; nevertheless, whenever this occurs and the term *TGNB* refers to a student or students, the possible deleted portion of the phrase *and/or gender questioning* is still applicable.

· LGBTQ, LGBTQ+, and LGBTQQIA+ (lesbian, gay, bisexual, transgender, queer, questioning, intersex, allies, plus others), or other variations, will be used as inclusive terms for anyone who identifies on the continuum; the term used is never meant to exclude or offend any person or group that identifies with one variation of this umbrella term over another. Its usage will reflect the details of the story or something specific to the passage.

· When deemed appropriate, the author may use material from her other workbooks that are part of this series.

· *This book does not provide medical or legal advice.* The information contained in this book is for informational purposes only. The opinions expressed in this book are those of the author, and any ideas or suggestions contained in the book are based solely on the author's experiences. This book is not intended to be a substitute for professional medical, mental health, or legal advice. Always seek the advice of your physician or other qualified healthcare/mental healthcare provider with any questions you may have regarding a medical condition, diagnosis, or treatment and before undertaking a new healthcare regimen. Never disregard professional medical advice or delay seeking it because of something you have read in this book. In addition, you should seek the advice of legal counsel familiar with the subject matter and authorized to practice in your jurisdiction before acting or relying on the opinions and information presented in this book.

CHAPTER SUMMARIES

Chapter 1 – Your Private Space: An Introduction

This chapter serves as an introduction that will explain the structure and purpose of the book. The workbook will provide a place free of judgment for you, the teacher and support staff, to reflect on your own journey and support your process of learning about and implementing best practices for those students who identify as transgender and/or non-binary. It is a self-reflective, private space where you can document any of your thoughts, feelings, fears, concerns, worries, confusions, pride, and celebrations in writing. Each of the following chapters will focus on one or two critical aspects of the transition process that may affect the daily school life of teachers, support staff, school administrators, and students.

Please note: Chapters 2-7 will contain passages that discuss experiences which relate to its title, followed by a combination of Anecdotal Affirmations, quizzes and exercises, graphic organizers, self-help stress ideas, empathic examples, Sampler Shares, and communication tools for school personnel. The chapters will also include specific questions to encourage Reflective Responses directly connected to the topics mentioned below.

Chapter 2 – Self-Reflecting When Concerned With What is Unfamiliar

This chapter will discuss the unknowns, apprehensive feelings, and misunderstandings teachers, support staff, and school administrators often express when they learn that a student in their school is transitioning and/or questioning their gender. It will address how to embrace TGNB students whether they identify on the binary or not and the appropriate ways to introduce the use of affirming pronouns and name changes. School personnel will be asked to take a clear look at their personal beliefs and reasons for them. Educators will also be challenged to understand how their own life experiences have shaped the philosophies that permeate their classroom on a daily basis. In addition, they will become aware of the ways these viewpoints and even subliminal messages impact all the students that they teach, including those who identify on the transgender spectrum and those who do not. Teachers, support staff, and school administrators will need to be honest with how they currently approach and interact with students who do not identify with the gender they were assigned at birth. By using the exercises and reflective questions, school personnel will be given an opportunity to search within themselves and formulate ways they can support those students who may not align with their personal viewpoints on gender identity and expression.

Chapter 3 – Do Social and Medical Changes Affect Privilege?

Learning how to accept potential changes can positively impact the school culture, as well as students' self-worth and confidence. This chapter will educate teachers, support staff, and school administrators about the difference between a social and medical transition. Within this framework, it will be necessary to untangle the misinformation and confusion that concerned educators have in relation to whether surgery will play a role in the lives of their students. Moreover, teachers, support staff, and school administrators will learn about a multitude of factors and options, such as hormone blockers, Tanner stages, and gender dysphoria, and gain many answers to their questions, while facing their own possible misconceptions. This chapter also explores if one's privilege is or has been affected through the intersections of patriarchy, misogyny, racism, transphobia, feminism, and male privilege. Furthermore, it will discuss how school policies and educators' practices may affect a loss of equality for those students who are in transition, do not identify along the binary, and/or are questioning their gender. In addition, this chapter will address the importance of school policies in regard to TGNB and/or gender questioning students possibly being excluded from specific social events or not being offered future opportunities that may foster an inherent loss or gain of participation in team sports, club memberships, school activities, and gendered parties. School personnel will question whether students' experiences within the school system ensure positive gains such as an increase of physical safety due to their transition.

Chapter 4 – Talking to Parents and Students

Knowing the legal rights and laws in your state/country and policies of the school district is critical for students and parents of TGNB and/or gender questioning students. It is essential that those working in school settings are educated about these facts. Having this knowledge and then hearing the desires of parents and students will enable teachers, support staff, and school administrators to honor the needs of the TGNB and/or gender questioning students in their school. In addition, it will empower educators to respond appropriately and correctly should they be questioned by those outside the TGNB and/or gender questioning student's family, including those families whose children do not identify as TGNB and/or gender questioning. It is equally important to discuss whether or not families of TGNB students elect to share this information with anyone else connected to the school. The exercises and tools within this chapter will help school personnel understand their own comfort level when confronted with questions and the options they have, should there be a need to discuss this information. Many times, concerns can be alleviated if the students and/or family members consult with a knowledgeable and experienced counselor. For some, the search for an appropriate therapist can be time consuming and vital. This chapter will also focus on the most applicable and best options for teachers and school administrators to offer if and when a TGNB student and/or family looks to the school district to provide outreach resources and/or school personnel to help them with their own journey. The activities within this chapter will aid those working in schools to create appropriate responses that align with school policies.

Chapter 5 – Behaviors, Bullying, Sports, and Bathrooms: It Takes a Village

Feeling safe and protected is a basic human need that a school can offer students. This chapter will discuss that this right is paramount for the TGNB and/or gender questioning students who attend school. Schools will be asked to review policies and procedures by responding to specific questions and exercises in relation to guidelines which often affect the safety and protection of their TGNB and/or gender questioning students. Teachers, support staff, and school administrators will be challenged to examine how they will ensure appropriate responses to inappropriate behaviors. Educators will learn how to recognize and deal with possible blatant and subtle bullying and harassment among students and faculty alike. Lastly, bathroom use and locker room issues will be considered and questioned to guarantee both the dignity and rights of the students they affect. This chapter will also incorporate the importance of training for all school personnel.

Chapter 6 – Viewing Practices and Curriculum While Creating a Culture of Inclusion

After assessing their present practices, teachers and support staff will have an opportunity to view their current curriculum through a new lens. They will be urged to examine what they can easily alter and implement based on essential exercises and the offering of Sampler Shares that ask them to stretch beyond their comfort zone in a private and risk-free experience when journaling. This chapter will afford clear and practical suggestions that are easy to incorporate in any classroom and school environment, hoping that these recommendations become a natural part of the school culture. In addition, teachers and support staff will be encouraged to evaluate the culture of their school classrooms and in some cases, shift their mindset in order to ensure the respectful inclusion of TGNB and/or gender questioning students in their school, especially those they instruct. This chapter also teaches educators how to welcome new ideas and say goodbye to old ones. In time, by using the exercises, tools, and questions within this chapter, these changes will ignite a culture that embraces the needs of all students, including those who identify on the transgender spectrum and/or are questioning their gender.

Chapter 7 – Celebrating the Changes and Passing on the Message

Changing your way of thinking or simply approaching something from a different perspective is often very difficult to do. This can be especially challenging for those who interact with students and school personnel, for everyone brings their own histories and biases to the table. Knowing this, it is extremely important to acknowledge and celebrate those who are able to make paradigm shifts. This chapter uses exercises and a variety of tools to recognize and applaud this mindset. By enabling school personnel to celebrate where they are now, how they have evolved, and what they have learned in regard to working with TGNB and/or gender questioning students in their classrooms and in the school, everyone can benefit. After using many of the activities offered in this workbook, teachers, support staff, and school administrators will have gained valuable knowledge and skills, but it is critical that educators do not remain complacent. School personnel should continue checking in and sharing both their celebrations and challenges with others in relation to trans issues, as they arise in and out of the classroom. It is important and helpful to revisit the tools, questions, and exercises in this chapter and all the others found within this workbook. As lifelong learners, educators are encouraged to research new materials and current laws, reassess and evaluate procedures, and stay abreast of any changes in language regarding the Trans community. This chapter will also discuss the importance of being aware that current school procedures may need to be updated periodically and why follow-through and continuous training will be necessary for all school personnel.

Chapter 8 – Resources, Answer Keys, and Glossary...Oh, My!

The last chapter will offer articles, books, blogs, camps, conferences, documentaries, films, music, support groups, websites, and more that focus on the needs of teachers, school administrators, and the students who identify on the transgender spectrum and/or are questioning their gender. It will also include a Glossary and all of the Answer Keys.

SET-UP

Each chapter will contain most, if not all, of the following sections.

1. Anecdotal Affirmations

These are poetic, appear throughout each chapter, and were created for you. They are meant to inspire, provoke thought, and empower your learning in any way that opens your heart. Their presence is intended to set the tone and intention of the chapter. The affirmations may be used as a springboard for writing or as a conversation starter with someone else.

2. Vital Vignettes

These serve as an introduction to the questions. The vignettes are included to help you gain some insight as you learn about how to support and accept the TGNB and/or gender questioning students in your school. Providing these passages as a precursor to the questions is meant to offer reflective thoughts of those who freely, but anonymously, shared their stories with me during the interviews and workshops that I have led and attended. Quite often they represent some of the experiences I have encountered as a teacher in the hope of communicating what I have witnessed or learned in order to be of assistance to you as you embark on this educational journey to help the needs of TGNB and/or gender questioning students in your school.

3. Graphics Galore

The chapters in this book will contain graphic organizers that can be used to assist you in expressing your thoughts without having to write them in a narrative format. In order to serve you best, they may be placed in a specific order within each chapter. Every graphic organizer can be used for various purposes, but if you find one type works best for you, use it as often as you like.

Bar Graph is an image that can be viewed to observe the ranking of data, which is translated into bar-like structures to display findings on a topic or question. Through the illustrations of the gathered information, the user can evaluate the comparison of the bars to reach their own conclusions in reference to a single topic or question. This graphic organizer encourages you to assess the importance or value of these topics, independent of the other topics, based on a personal rating system of 1–10. In contrast to the *Pie Graph* graphic organizer, although both organizers enable the user to view the topics in comparison with the others, the bars of the *Bar Graph* do not need to add up to 100 or 100 percent.

Box is a format for notes or can be used as a place to store information connected to one topic or subject, which compartmentalizes or assesses a situation. It is visually comprised of multiple boxes to create a framework.

Pie Graph is a visual representation of percentage showing the comparison of various categories based on a single subject, question, or circumstance in the shape of a pie. Some think of it as a pizza pie with each slice standing for a different component of the topic. The total composition of all the parts is summed to 100 or 100 percent. Each part or section is assigned a percentage based on its user's point of view. The goal is to exhibit a quick way to prioritize or place a value on every critical factor that affects the outcome of the subject, question, or circumstance in relation to the other topics.

Splash should be imagined as if you took a liquid, such as water or paint, and splattered it on a blank canvas. It is intended to let your juices flow as you brainstorm with no judgment or organizational care. Respond to the statement or inquiry with a word or short phrase and quickly splatter your reply. By creatively splashing words and short phrases, you will attempt to express your responses randomly by scattering them on paper. When you have completed the graphic organizer, it should almost look as if you have created a canvas of words by squirting them on the page. It encourages you to elicit a reaction that is visceral and has a desire to be released on paper.

T-Chart can be used to show different perspectives in relation to the same topic or question. There are many versions of this graphic organizer that can host two, three, or more columns. The graphic usually lists or states aspects of a problem, unknown, or dilemma. This workbook contains the three- and four-column *T-Chart* format that can assist the user in documenting information. One variation of this type of organizer is KWL, which houses what a person "Knows," "Wants to know or learn," and then does "Learn."

Timeline is sequential and helps record the order or timing of a situation or event that has or will occur. Though not used in its traditional format, it assists in creating a tentative time frame to complete a current or future task that may be time sensitive with numerous factors or parts.

Venn Diagram is a graphic organizer that aids in comparing and contrasting a situation or an inquiry. Once a question is posed, one side of the connecting circles is filled in with one point of view. Then the other side of the diagram is completed with the other response in relation to the same question, showing the reply to the inquiry from a different point of view. The last step is to notice if any of the replies from the two sides overlap. If any are the same or very similar, that response is removed from both sides and placed in the center-interlocking portion of the graphic organizer. The outcome is noticing where the responses agree and where they differ.

Webs are often described as presenting a topic and its subtopics in the way that a spider's web scatters branch-like patterns, which generate from a central source. Every part of the growing web is connected to an initial word or phrase. Once the beginning word or phrase is placed in the center position, the user's associated words or phrases are placed in the outer connecting circles in response to the central statement. This pattern continues until the web is completed or the response to the question or statement is personally finished.

4. Reflective Responses

There are several ways you can partake in the questions posed in this workbook, but ultimately the hope is for you to use them in the manner that works best for your needs. Some individuals may only choose to write their responses to a select group of questions in each chapter, whereas others may reply to each and every question. You may even elect to repeat this process more than once throughout the transition process. Each chapter poses questions that are intended to help you discover where you stand in regard to processing the transition and what is comfortable for you. Your responses may remain the same for a long period of time or they may evolve as you explore your options and have time to digest all that you are experiencing and feeling. Each and every path has its own value and purpose.

5. Deserving De-Stressing Delights

Each chapter offers structured ways to release any stress you may be experiencing as you explore this journey and enables you to direct your energy toward de-stressing by rewarding yourself in a loving and tender manner. Intentionally allowing yourself time to simply stop, breathe, and rest from journaling and processing is essential for your well-being. This section reminds you to carve out space to engage in activities that restore and rejuvenate you through self-care, which will help you feel pampered and nurtured.

6. Empathy-Embracing Exercises

This exercise is meant to help you gain an awareness of the importance of confronting any of your possible concerns and confusions while strengthening your acceptance level as students in your school transition or consider doing so. Perhaps thinking of a private and difficult experience from your past or in the present will create a deeper understanding of the emotional process TGNB and/or gender questioning students may be experiencing. Its inclusion in the workbook is to encourage you to view the transition through the lens of a TGNB and/or gender questioning student, while honoring your possible concerns and confusions in order to better prepare you for the process.

7. Sampler Shares

The samplers were created as a means to assist educators with ways they can embrace and support the students in their class who identify as transgender, non-binary and/or are questioning their gender. I am submitting some of my own sample replies to several of the questions in this workbook, hoping to inspire you to use them as a springboard to formulate your own practices. They are included simply to open your mind to a variety of ways to incorporate positive change in your classroom or within the school setting for those students who identify as transgender, non-binary, and gender questioning, as well as for those who do not. Though most of the Sampler Shares refer to experiences involving TGNB and/or gender questioning students, some are included to show there are dozens of school lessons, activities, events, and policies rooted in gender-based practices that occur more from habit than necessity or any educational value. However, the purpose of their presence in this section is to provide awareness of how gender-based practices may play a role in your classroom and school, impacting a multitude of students regardless of their gender identity.

8. Communication Corner

This exercise was designed with the intention of offering teachers, support staff, and administrators a safe place to discuss all the topics addressed in the chapter. When two or more school employees candidly begin a conversation that embraces an open dialogue without judgment or criticism of one another's thoughts and ideas concerning students and school policies, everyone benefits. It is suggested that after teachers, support staff, and administrators privately answer the questions from the Reflective Responses section, they converse about one or two of them, while others may prefer to answer them all with a trusted colleague or administrator.

All pages marked with ★ can be photocopied and downloaded at
https://library.jkp.com/redeem using the code TLVNEKN

QUESTION #1

Before you proceed to Chapter 2, I invite you to respond to the following question:

What do you hope or expect to learn or gain from reading and journaling in this workbook?

....

....

....

....

....

....

....

....

....

....

....

....

....

....

....

....

....

Chapter 2

SELF-REFLECTING WHEN CONCERNED WITH WHAT IS UNFAMILIAR

VITAL VIGNETTE

As professionals, teachers and support staff experience much pride in helping students feel protected, understood, and valued. Extending this care to TGNB and/or gender questioning students should be no exception. Since many educators may not be familiar with the needs of these students, those who teach and interact with TGNB and/or gender questioning students can be at a loss in knowing how to best serve them at school. One essential distinction that must be understood by all school personnel is that gender and sexuality are different from one another, but they are interrelated. Gender is how a person internally experiences themselves as male, female, masculine, feminine, some combination of these, or none of them; aspects of these can be culturally defined. Sexuality is the pattern of thoughts, feelings, and arousal that determine sexual preferences. For the purposes of this book, whenever sexuality is mentioned, it is specifically referring to sexual orientation that is described as: to whom a person is attracted and/or with whom they want to have sex. Gaining this insight, should it not be previously known, will assist all those who work in schools to become better informed in terms of TGNB and/or gender questioning students. There are several simple but vital actions teachers and support staff can implement to assure the comfort and acceptance of TGNB and/or gender questioning students. As these details are being introduced, it is also important to be aware that special needs students and/or those on the autism spectrum can also identify on the transgender spectrum and/or be questioning their gender.

Knowing pronouns and names are major parts of any person's identity, it is imperative to realize that this is especially true for students who are trans. Though pronouns and names used to refer to or about an individual may seem insignificant to some, it is extremely important to TGNB and/or gender questioning people. Recognizing their need to be acknowledged with the pronoun and name that align with their affirmed gender will show a great deal of respect. It is a good practice for all those who work in schools to ask all students and co-workers what pronoun/s and names they want others to use when referring to or discussing them. For some TGNB and/or gender questioning students, selecting a pronoun and name can be a challenging task, but for others, it will be extremely clear. The pronoun options educators are most familiar with are *she/her/hers* and *he/him/his* that signify purely binary choices; whereas, *they/them/their* is also commonly used as a singular pronoun in and out of the Trans community. Moreover, some students may be comfortable using more than one pronoun for themselves or not having a pronoun preference. This may be a foreign concept to grasp for teachers, support staff, administrators, and even students, especially for those who are not aware of these possibilities; however, this cannot be a deterrent for not honoring a student's need.

For example, a student who uses *she/her/hers* pronouns, "She is driving her mom to the conference," would be the traditional statement. However, students may desire to use their affirmed name for their pronoun. For those who use their affirmed name for their pronoun, this statement would be reworded as, "Whitney is driving Whitney's mom to the conference." Furthermore, for those who use *they/their/them* pronouns, the sentence should be worded, "They are driving their mom to the conference." There are individuals who have expressed that using *they/them/their* pronouns is not grammatically correct. Others have shared that *they/them/their* pronouns sound "weird" or "wrong." In many Trans communities it is understood that there is a learning curve when incorporating a different pronoun that aligns with a student's affirmed gender. Nevertheless, it is unacceptable to judge or insult students when they are using pronouns that best affirm their gender. With the willingness and ample time to practice, using *they/their/them* pronouns or a person's affirmed name for their pronoun can become as natural as using *she/her/hers* and *he/him/his*. Unintentional mistakes will occur and this is all par for the course. Regardless, purposely using the wrong pronoun is improper. Making a sincere effort to validate a student's affirming pronoun/s, whether they identify as TGNB or not, will mean more to these individuals than you could possibly imagine.

As students transition and/or are questioning their gender, their name and/or pronoun/s may also be in transition and/or fluid. It is understandable that this can be perplexing for educators; therefore it is all the more critical they remain open-minded. It is suggested that teachers and support staff create an atmosphere that provides a safe space for TGNB and/or gender questioning students to be able to convey their need for these changes. Once the pronoun shift is confirmed, there needs to be a specific policy on how a teacher will network this new information to all school personnel. This process should also hold true when a student requires to be addressed by a name other than the one assigned at birth. Though some schools elect to not recognize a student by their affirmed name and/or pronoun/s, unless it has been legally changed, many schools will honor these wishes without any official documentation. In some instances, schools will request that parents communicate these changes in writing, whereas other schools will accept a student's appeal to do so without parental consent or any opposition.

One simple but meaningful way all those who work in schools can clearly show solidarity with TGNB and/or gender questioning students and faculty is to list your pronouns after your name when it is visually displayed in email and/or exhibited in other online platforms where pronouns are relevant in connection to an individual's name, in such a manner as: D. M. Maynard (She/Her/Hers), Chris Smith (He/Him/His), or Sam Blake

(They/Them/Theirs), etc. If verbally stating your name as part of your introduction, it is strongly suggested that all those associated with the school population also include their pronouns. By following this respectful action, TGNB and/or gender questioning students and faculty will have the burden removed from the equation of being the only ones having to declare their pronoun/s once this preferred practice becomes more common and accepted by all.

Educators often apply their own life experiences to situations when they are learning something new. If this information is part of a teacher or support staff's history, it may be easier to absorb and integrate into practice. When this material is not familiar to an educator and/or contradicts their beliefs, issuing a directive to incorporate this knowledge into their daily teaching can become extremely challenging. The reason for this cognitive dissonance may not be known but it will need to be addressed in order for school personnel to best serve all students.

Many of the apprehensive thoughts teachers and support staff may be internalizing can be based on the fear of unknowns and unanswered questions. What does it mean to socially transition? Can medical interventions be part of a student's transition? What is appropriate to say or ask TGNB students and their parents? What am I permitted to share with other students and their parents? How can I protect TGNB and/or gender questioning students from being bullied and harassed in school? What are the bathroom, locker room, team sports, and related concerns pertaining to school policies? Whom do I ask when I do not know the correct response to inquiries in relation to trans rights? How can I learn to accept TGNB and/or gender questioning students in my school if it conflicts with my religious faith? If I suspect a student is questioning their gender but is not verbalizing it to me, what do I do? Am I required to inform a family member and/or administrator if a student confides in me that they are questioning their gender and/or now identifies as TGNB? How can I best be an ally to TGNB and/or gender questioning students? What is the proper protocol if a colleague becomes hostile toward a student, or me, for supporting a student's affirmed gender? How can I incorporate appropriate lessons that empower TGNB and/or gender questioning students?

These are a small sample of concerns and questions all school personnel may be asking themselves as they begin to learn how to address the needs of TGNB and/or gender questioning students. The answers to these ponderings can have a major effect on the lives of TGNB and/or gender questioning students in your school. They may also shape your philosophies and impact your teaching. How you decide to approach these unknowns can influence the way students in your classroom react to and interact with TGNB and/or gender questioning students in your school. It may also play a key role in whether TGNB and/or gender questioning students feel safe in their environment, free to be themselves, and are respected by peers. It is necessary for teachers and support staff, as well as administrators, to be honest with themselves and reflect on their own possible personal conflicts or opposing beliefs. Doing so can ensure that TGNB and/or gender questioning students are treated fairly and appropriately while under your care.

The responses to most of your questions will be addressed within the contents of this workbook. The exercises, graphic organizers, and suggestions aim to assist you in finding your own voice, sorting out any confusions, and searching for novel ways of helping TGNB and/or gender questioning students in your school. Your acceptance can make all the difference to a student. The path you will travel as an educator in serving TGNB and/or gender questioning students you meet along the way will not always be easy. It is crucial to acknowledge that you may not be able to accomplish every well-intentioned goal. Yet, knowing that your support will never be forgotten and that you are laying the foundation for a positive educational experience for all TGNB and/or gender questioning students in the future, will be reason enough to embark on this journey and enable you to learn the most impactful lessons of a lifetime.

ANECDOTAL AFFIRMATION

ANECDOTAL AFFIRMATION

*We may not
Know why,
But we know
Change is
Going to happen.*

This Anecdotal Affirmation is meant to inspire, provoke thought, and empower your learning in any way that opens your heart. Its presence is intended to set the tone and intention of the chapter. This affirmation may be used as a springboard for writing or as a conversation starter with someone else. Ample space has been provided for you to reflect on the Anecdotal Affirmation.

GRAPHICS GALORE

Splash

Can you jot down all the words and terms that connect to the Transgender (Trans) community? As you brainstorm, write your words and terms quickly by randomly scattering them anywhere on the page in a splash-like manner. Use the information obtained from the *Splash* to assess what words and terms you already know in relation to the Trans community.

REFLECTIVE RESPONSES

1. What is your experience working with TGNB and/or gender questioning students?

. . . .

. . . .

. . . .

. . . .

. . . .

. . . .

. . . .

2. How do you feel about the directive to support TGNB and/or gender questioning students in your classroom and/or school?

. . . .

. . . .

. . . .

. . . .

. . . .

. . . .

. . . .

3. What teachings from your upbringing, if any, do you believe have shaped your inner beliefs, feelings, and practices in relation to accepting TGNB and/or gender questioning students in your classroom and/or school?

....

....

....

....

....

....

....

....

4. What teachings from your upbringing, if any, do you believe have shaped your inner beliefs, feelings, and practices in relation to not accepting TGNB and/or gender questioning students in your classroom and/or school?

....

....

....

....

....

....

....

5. What experiences from your life, if any, enable you to easily support or make it challenging for you to embrace the journeys of TGNB and/or gender questioning students?

....

....

....

....

....

....

....

6. How do you feel that addressing the needs of TGNB and/or gender questioning students will or will not affect your teaching?

....

....

....

....

....

....

....

7. How have you responded to a directive or request from an authoritative figure that did not align with your beliefs or was not to your liking?

....

....

....

....

....

....

....

....

8. What questions do you have in relation to TGNB and/or gender questioning students in your classroom and/or school?

....

....

....

....

....

....

....

....

9. What are your concerns, if any, in relation to TGNB and/or gender questioning students in your classroom and/or school?

....

....

....

....

....

....

....

....

10. What educational philosophies do you currently hold that may impact the lives of TGNB and/or gender questioning students in your classroom and/or school?

....

....

....

....

....

....

....

....

11. How have your school colleagues responded to the TGNB and/or gender questioning students in your classroom and/or school?

....

....

....

....

....

....

....

....

12. How have your school administrators responded to TGNB and/or gender questioning students in your classroom and/or school?

....

....

....

....

....

....

....

....

GAME

Matching Pre-Test 1

It is important to be aware of what you know and to use that knowledge as a starting point to grow. After taking the pre-test, you will realize what you still need to learn. The tools in this chapter were created to help you internalize the vocabulary. As a pre-test, match the vocabulary (the numbers) with the definitions (the letters) by drawing a line from a number to a letter. Each number and letter should only be used once. What were your results? The answer keys are provided in the Answer Key section in Chapter 8. It is suggested that you check your answers after you have taken the pre-test to see how well you did. Feel free to repeat this process at a later time; you may choose to use this activity to assess your progress by using this game as a post-test.

Vocabulary	Definition
1. AFAB	A. Someone who does not feel sexual attraction to other people.
2. agender	B. A person who is attracted to both masculine and feminine people.
3. AMAB	C. An abbreviation that stands for an individual who was assigned female at birth by a medical doctor based on the visible appearance of their genitalia at birth.
4. androgynous	D. Someone who does not identify with any gender.
5. asexual	E. The belief that there are only two genders: male and female.
6. bigender	F. A surgical procedure that permanently changes the genitals or internal reproductive organs.
7. bilateral mastectomy	G. Someone who possesses both masculine and feminine characteristics.
8. binary	H. A surgical procedure that removes breast tissue from both sides of the chest and can include the construction of a male-appearing chest.
9. binding	I. It can designate a number of sexual orientations and possibilities that are not mutually exclusive and may also refer to someone assigned female at birth but who does not identify as, or only partially identifies as, a girl or woman; moreover, they often identify as lesbians, dykes, or queer.
10. bisexual (bi)	J. An abbreviation that stands for an individual who was assigned male at birth by a medical doctor based on the visible appearance of their genitalia at birth.
11. boi	K. Someone who experiences themselves as both masculine and feminine.
12. bottom surgery	L. A practice of using material or clothing to constrict the breasts that enables a person to flatten their chest.

Retake this pre-test as a post-test to assess your personal progress and knowledge.

EMPATHY-EMBRACING EXERCISE

Part of a teacher, support staff, or administrator's journey may involve adjusting to using a student's affirmed name and/or pronoun/s. The following questions show teachers, support staff, and administrators that accommodating a name change is a common experience for many people. The greatest learning tools for grasping the change in name and/or pronoun/s are patience with yourself, willingness, time, and much practice.

Do you know anyone from your past who has asked you to call them by a different name, pronoun, or honorific, perhaps due to marriage or for other reasons? How long did it take you to adjust to this new name, pronoun, or honorific, and how did you learn to adjust to the change?

GRAPHICS GALORE

Web

Understanding that for some teachers and support staff, learning how to appropriately serve those students who identify as TGNB and/or gender questioning may be concerning and confusing. This graphic organizer provides a space for you to record your questions. These inquiries can help you feel prepared, should you need to address these thoughts during training courses, when doing research, or if the opportunity presents itself. What are some of the confusing or concerning questions you may have in regard to understanding how you can appropriately serve TGNB and/or gender questioning students?

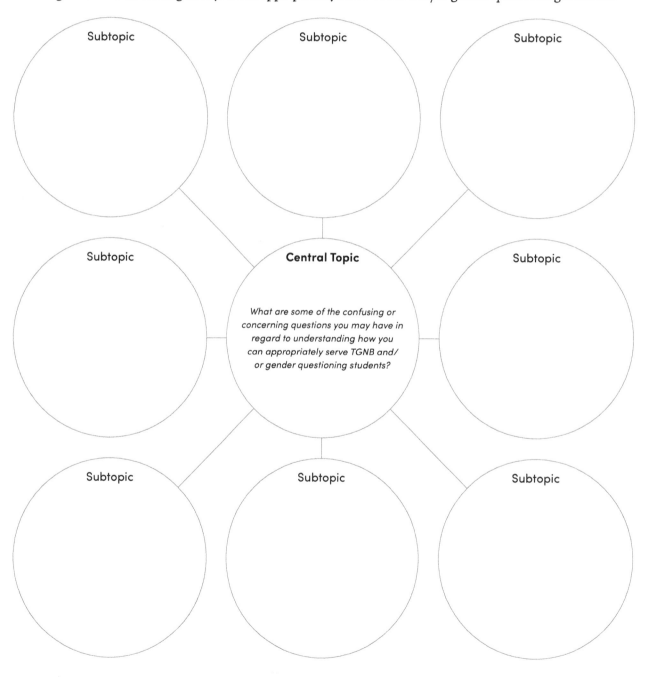

DESERVING DE-STRESSING DELIGHT

Meditation, Reading, and Writing

Relaxing your mind and body at a time of stress can be very helpful in providing clarity and calmness. Many educators and support staff may find meditation in any form to be extremely comforting to quiet some of their concerns and fears in relation to the unknown and to the transition process that may face their students. The following are other ways you can find solace and tranquility. Sometimes walking in an active and noisy area can awaken your senses of sight and hearing and enable you to block out all the conflicting thoughts, ideas, and worries in your head, helping you to be an observer of your environment. Horns beeping, doors slamming, and people talking can become music to your ears and surprisingly soothing.

In contrast, others may adore the beauty and solitude of the beach and may not even realize how emotionally cathartic it can be to listen to the water and appreciate nature. For many people, hearing the ocean and looking at the sunset can offer a feeling of peace as they sort things out. For some, hiking and walking in the woods or taking a stroll on new, pristine snow can bring them much serenity. Yet others find peace and comfort attending support groups, religious services, or speaking with a spiritual mentor. If you want a more structured approach to practice stillness, you can attend a meditation class. Listening to a guided audiotape, peaceful music, or participating in a gentle yoga class can also feel relaxing. These experiences may allow you to be passive as you receive the directed suggestions. It could be calming to close your eyes and embrace the gentleness of harmonious sounds. If walking or being guided by an outside entity does not seem to be what you need, you may seek out an activity that is both repetitive and mindless, such as doing a jigsaw puzzle, a word search, or simply coloring or sketching.

For many, there can be a quietness that takes over a person's entire body when they pick up a warm cup of tea or coffee and curl up with a good book. Reading allows some people to block out their stress by venturing into a land of make-believe. Some days there is no better remedy than a book or writing your thoughts in a journal. Reading or writing can transport a person to a place of imagination and reflection. It is like being in the presence of a trusted friend who is simply there to listen and comfort you without any demands. When the pressures of your job are nonstop, reading and writing may be the first course of action and even after a bit of time can still do the trick and help you unwind. If reading is pleasurable for you, it is suggested that you snuggle up with a book based on the genre of your liking, with a beverage and/or snack of choice, in a location that feels lovely to you. Should writing be more relaxing for you, feel free to use pages in this workbook or purchase a special journal and with your favorite writing utensil begin the soothing process of writing for yourself, just for fun and without any judgment. If both reading and writing appeal to you, then indulge in both and enjoy!

Most de-stressing for some is taking a mini-nap. You could set an alarm for 20–30 minutes and close your eyes as you sit in a chair or lie on a bed. Often, repeating a mantra or imagining yourself in a specific place that you love and just letting yourself breathe

deeply will reduce tension. When the time is up, you can feel renewed and ready to face the world of things that are familiar or unfamiliar!

Journal your reaction to this Deserving De-Stressing Delight.

Word Search

```
G S A B A F A Q A B O I E S R E V I D R E D N E G
S R E K C O L B Y T R E B U P X F A M I L I E S R
N Y D I L A T E C N G T A S E G A T S R E N N A T
S T H E Y D G N I M R O F N O C N O N R E D N E G
M T M S U O N Y G O R D N A G A T E K E E P E R S
S G E N D E R M A R K E R S S U O P E H R N G I Y
N K W T I T W O S P I R I T G N I T U O Y S A C N
U G A R D V T T R A C H E A L S H A V E R B D I Y
O M P A X C R C Q T B G L T O P S U R G E R Y S G
N E A N G J A E F S U O R O M A Y L O P G G P G O
O T N S N R N T R E B I N D I N G R L H R A Y E S
R O H I I Y S S E X S G N M X S V X A A U I T N I
P I Y D N T M A D U Y Q H T A E U N U L S R I D M
R D S E O S I M N A D U E F H X G T X L M O T E V
E I T N I A S L E L K E L M E U B R E O O H N R A
D O E T T L O A G I O E Q S R A I A S P T P E P G
N P R I I P G R S T U R A V X L G P A L T S D R I
E L E F S O Y E N Y I N T E R S E X R A O Y I I N
G A C I N T N T A Y A M A B R Z N C O S B D R V O
D S T E A O Y A R S T N E R A P D V S T W R E I P
E T O D R R M L T N P F H T L A E T S Y A E D L L
R Y M O T C E I H C R O B I N A R Y D I O D N E A
R G Y C I S P B K G L R E D N E G A R Q E N E G S
E Y R E G R U S G N I M R I F F A R E D N E G E T
F A C I A L F E M I N I Z A T I O N S U R G E R Y
E F T M S U O M A G O N O M F N O E M A N D A E D
R R E E U Q R E D N E G Y T C I S G E N D E R Z W
P A S S I N G R E D N E G D I U L F R E D N E G O
G N I K C A P G E N D E R E X P R E S S I O N Z G
P L A U X E S S N A R T A S D F Y R A N I B N O N
E J B I S E X U A L T S I G O L O N I R C O D N E
Z G N I N O I T S E U Q X T R A N S P H O B I A Z
B I N T E R S E C T I O N A L I T Y X N G T G N B
C O P C O M P E R S I O N S N A R T R E N T R A P
```

How many of the words, listed on the next page, can you find in this Word Search?

Can you find these bonus words not listed on the next page: FAMILIES, PARENTS, and TRANS?

The answer key for the Word Search is in the Answer Key section in Chapter 8. Good luck and have fun!

Words for Word Search

AFAB	endocrinologist	LGBTQ	queer
agender	facial feminization surgery	metoidioplasty	questioning
AMAB	FTM/MTM	misogyny	scrotoplasty
androgynous	gatekeeper	monogamous	sexuality
asexual	gender	MTF/FTF	stealth
bigender	gender-affirming surgery	non-binary	Tanner stages
bilateral mastectomy	gender diverse	orchiectomy	TGNB
binary	gender dysphoria	outing	TGNC
binding	gender expression	packing	they
bisexual	gender fluid	pan hysterectomy	top surgery
boi	gender identity	pansexual	tracheal shave
bottom surgery	gender marker	partner	transgender/ trans-identified
cisgender	gender non-conforming	passing	transitioning
cisgender privilege	genderqueer	phalloplasty	transmisogyny
compersion	GnRH	POC	transphobia
deadname	GSA	polyamorous	transsexual
dilate	intersectionality	preferred gender pronouns	two-spirit
drag	intersex	puberty blockers	vaginoplasty

GRAPHICS GALORE

Venn Diagram

List the behaviors and strengths you and/or society believe are uniquely common to masculinity and then uniquely common to femininity. Once this is completed, list those behaviors and strengths that overlap for both masculinity and femininity. Please note that it is extremely important to acknowledge and be aware of how these perceptions of gender binary behaviors and strengths affect those who identify as TGNB and/or gender questioning.

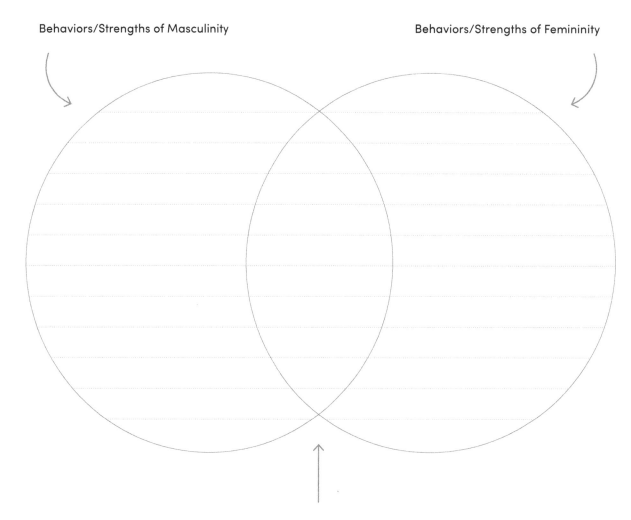

Behaviors/Strengths of Masculinity

Behaviors/Strengths of Femininity

Overlapping the Behaviors/Strengths of Masculinity
With the Behaviors/Strengths of Femininity

SAMPLER SHARE

I am submitting my own reply to the *Reflective Responses* question listed below as a sample, hoping to inspire you to use it as a springboard to formulate your own practices. Please be aware that all of the students' names have been removed, as well as most of the actual pronouns for the student and parent, in order to respect the privacy of TGNB and/or gender questioning students, their parents, and other family members. It should be noted that all of these methods can be beneficial for all students, not only those who identify as TGNB and/or are questioning their gender. It is imperative to understand that even without intending to, gender-based practices can negatively impact the social and emotional well-being of students who identify on the transgender spectrum. For these reasons and the need to be transparent, samples are incorporated that portray how the lives of gender-diverse students were also affected, though they did not identify themselves as TGNB and/or gender questioning at the time of the event. Whether they do now, or not, is unknown.

How do you feel about the directive to support TGNB and/or gender questioning students in your classroom and/or school?

Twice a year, students had the opportunity to participate in Photo Day. For years, I had simply brought my entire class to engage in this picture-taking ritual by forming two separate lines along the gender binary and then organizing my students according to their heights, from taller to shorter. I never gave it much thought, always knowing that I would be able to have this photo as a valued keepsake forever. As I became more aware of the needs of TGNB and/or gender questioning students, it became extremely clear how traumatic this semiannual event was for some of them. Realizing this and not understanding why this was a necessary directive, I questioned the photographer who told me that it was part of their tradition and to that I replied that it was now time to break this tradition. As we reconfigured our now single-line formation based solely on height, the photographer was not happy with me. Overhearing the annoyance in the voice of the photographer, the parent volunteer who organized Photo Day walked over to intervene. I privately explained my reason for refusing to create two binary lines and much to my delight, the volunteer supported my action. The following year on Photo Day, the students in my class formed only one line according to height, instead of two that once considered gender. This was the first of many times I found myself questioning directives that impeded the emotional well-being of TGNB and/or gender questioning students!

GRAPHICS GALORE

Pie Graph

Decide how significant these issues are to you in relation to each other. Place the number that corresponds with a suggested topic within as many slices of the pie that conveys how each one matters to you. Only one number should be placed in each slice. You do not need to use all the issues, but do fill in all the slices. Feel free to create your own topics and assign them their own number. It is critical that educators process and reflect on their feelings about these crucial policies that will continue to affect the lives of students who identify as TGNB and/or are questioning their gender. More importantly, educators must overcome their own possible conflicting beliefs to ensure that they always treat all students with the dignity and respect they deserve.

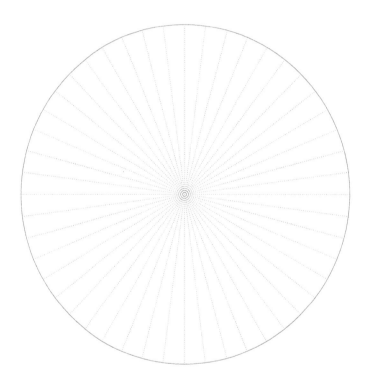

To what degree are these policy concerns and related topics important to you? Concern that...

1. TGNB students will not be safe in bathrooms and locker rooms at school, based on their affirmed gender.

2. TGNB students will not be safe at school in other locations, in addition to bathrooms and locker rooms.

3. TGNB students will not be welcome to participate in afterschool programs, clubs, sports, parties, and other activities, if they request to do so while living in their affirmed gender.

4. All school personnel, students, and parents will not receive proper training in relation to how to incorporate the needs of TGNB students in your school.

5. School personnel will not agree to follow all laws and school policies in relation to honoring the needs of TGNB students.

6. School personnel will not agree to honor the use of TGNB students' gender affirming name and pronoun/s.

7. School personnel will not agree to change TGNB students' gender affirming name, pronoun/s, and gender marker on all school documents and records.

8. School personnel will not be adequately prepared in regard to social and/or medical aspects of transitioning in relation to TGNB students.

9. School personnel will not be familiar with appropriate terms and/or vocabulary related to the Trans community.

10. School personnel, students, and parents will not be respectful and accepting of TGNB students in your school.

ANECDOTAL AFFIRMATION

ANECDOTAL AFFIRMATION

Ask questions,
Get answers,
Keep asking
More questions!

This Anecdotal Affirmation is meant to inspire, provoke thought, and empower your learning in any way that opens your heart. Its presence is intended to set the tone and intention of the chapter. This affirmation may be used as a springboard for writing or as a conversation starter with someone else. Ample space has been provided for you to reflect on the Anecdotal Affirmation.

COMMUNICATION CORNER

Reflecting on your own thoughts and experiences is critical when processing new information and adjusting your thinking. Equally important can be sharing and learning how others analyze their own thoughts and experiences. This exercise was designed with the intention of offering teachers, support staff, and administrators a safe place to discuss all the topics addressed in this chapter. When two or more school employees candidly begin a conversation that embraces an open dialogue without judgment or criticism of one another's beliefs and ideas concerning students and school policies, everyone benefits. It is suggested that after teachers, support staff, and administrators privately answer the questions from the Reflective Responses section, they converse about one or two of them, while others may prefer to answer them all with a trusted colleague or administrator. In order to recall the questions you answered, simply highlight or circle the ones you addressed and then ask others the ones they responded to on their own. By doing so in a respectful and communicative manner that honors the voices of all those working or interacting with the students who identify as transgender, non-binary, and/or are questioning their gender, teachers, support staff, and administrators in your school can positively impact the lives of the students they are committed to serve as professionals. Do you and your colleague or administrator answer these questions in the same way or differently? Discuss your responses to understand how all of you view the answers to the questions and make time to celebrate all you learn from being willing to communicate with one another.

1. What is your experience working with TGNB and/or gender questioning students?

. . . .

. . . .

2. How do you feel about the directive to support TGNB and/or gender questioning students in your classroom and/or school?

. . . .

. . . .

3. What teachings from your upbringing, if any, do you believe have shaped your inner beliefs, feelings, and practices in relation to accepting TGNB and/or gender questioning students in your classroom and/or school?

. . . .

. . . .

4. What teachings from your upbringing, if any, do you believe have shaped your inner beliefs, feelings, and practices in relation to not accepting TGNB and/ or gender questioning students in your classroom and/or school?

....

....

5. What experiences from your life, if any, enable you to easily support or make it challenging for you to embrace the journeys of TGNB and/or gender questioning students?

....

....

6. How do you feel that addressing the needs of TGNB and/or gender questioning students will or will not affect your teaching?

....

....

7. How have you responded to a directive or request from an authoritative figure that did not align with your beliefs or was not to your liking?

....

....

8. What questions do you have in relation to TGNB and/or gender questioning students in your classroom and/or school?

....

....

9. What are your concerns, if any, in relation to TGNB and/or gender questioning students in your classroom and/or school?

....

....

10. What educational philosophies do you currently hold that may impact the lives of TGNB and/or gender questioning students in your classroom and/or school?

. . . .

. . . .

11. How have your school colleagues responded to the TGNB and/or gender questioning students in your classroom and/or school?

. . . .

. . . .

12. How have your school administrators responded to TGNB and/or gender questioning students in your classroom and/or school?

. . . .

. . . .

Chapter 3

DO SOCIAL AND MEDICAL CHANGES AFFECT PRIVILEGE?

VITAL VIGNETTE

For some educators, their first experience of knowing someone who is transitioning and/or questioning their gender occurs when their student self-identifies on the transgender spectrum. For many, this can be an unfamiliar area. Teachers, support staff, and administrators may have questions to ask and not be sure where to turn in order to gather information and gain knowledge. If and when a student transitions and/or is questioning their gender, two major aspects will be introduced: socially transitioning and medically transitioning. If a student is under legal age, their parents or others legally responsible for the student's welfare will also be involved with both the process and decision making in relation to the outcome. In many instances, a key difference between socially transitioning and medically transitioning is that most social interventions can easily be implemented or reversed on their own, whereas a large majority of medical interventions would require trained and highly skilled professional assistance in making any changes.

To help untangle misinformation, most young students who identify on the transgender spectrum and/or are questioning their gender begin their process by socially transitioning. Socially transitioning can be in an abundance of forms and in most cases these changes are not invasive. If this aspect is part of a student's journey, there is no specific order in which any of the social interventions need to occur. Each student, ideally with the involvement of an adult legally responsible for their care, will determine for themselves which, if any, options feel correct for them. Since a large number of students may be discovering what feels right for them, these factors may be adjusted throughout the transition process. It is critical that school personnel honor this process by providing flexibility as students and their families travel this path.

This, too, applies to TGNB youth and dating. Though it was mentioned in the previous chapter that gender and sexuality are not the same, it is essential to note that they can be interconnected. Dating for TGNB and/or gender questioning students, just as for cisgender (someone whose gender assigned at birth and gender identity are aligned) students in school, may be somewhat complex. This can be especially valid for some students who are trans-identified and/or questioning their gender, yet this may not be true for all. It is important for those working in schools to understand that the sexual orientation of TGNB and/or gender questioning students can be fluid, and if this occurs, their choices must be respected.

For some students, changing their pronoun to align with their affirmed gender can be an extremely vital part of their social transition. This is also true for their name. As discussed previously, whether this is done legally or not, having those in the school setting honor these two simple modifications can have an enormous, positive, and emotional effect on a TGNB student's daily life. It is crucial that these changes be reflected in any location where they will be posted or viewed. When applicable, teachers and support staff will need to remember to include and clearly state the affirmed name and pronoun in substitute plans, field-trip and take-home forms, report card comments, library book check-out materials, medical records, instructional groupings and displays around the classroom and hallway, for login purposes, picture day information, on lunchroom slips, in after-school programs, and for anything connected to recess.

Dressing or wearing their hair in a manner that aligns with a student's affirmed gender can be a physical type of adjustment that helps a student feel at ease with their body and it is also quite helpful in reducing their gender dysphoria. Gender dysphoria is the uncomfortable, distressing, anxiety-provoking, and sometimes depressing feelings that occur in people when aspects of their body and behavior are not congruent with their gender identity. Dressing or styling their hair in a way that empowers them to accurately express their affirmed gender can also offer visual cues, which enable a student to be seen properly and may prevent TGNB students from being gendered incorrectly. Clothing can also be an obstacle for TGNB and/or gender questioning students who attend schools, participate in certain clubs, or play on sports teams that require specific uniforms based on gender. These strict guidelines can discourage or prevent TGNB and/or gender questioning students from joining these organizations.

For those students who identify as non-binary, their affirmed gender may not align with the binary options often imposed on students in Western culture. As a result, though a non-binary student may dress or style their hair in a manner that is being true to and representative of themselves, school personnel may incorrectly gender a student and this can be emotionally devastating to them. Instead of attempting to guess a student's affirmed gender when using pronouns or names, based on their way of dressing, it is always best to ask that student privately which pronoun and name they use. If an unintentional error occurs, apologize for the mistake, take responsibility, and correct it without placing any judgment or blame on the student. Moreover, never ignore the situation and feel it did not matter, because it most likely will pain the student on many levels. It is a learning curve and mistakes will happen, but how teachers, support staff, and administrators react to the error can have a positive or negative lingering effect on a student. Consequently, if another student or a colleague genders a student incorrectly, it may be appropriate for you to rise to the occasion and politely correct their error. However, it is imperative to note that many TGNB and/or gender questioning students are quite comfortable advocating for themselves in these moments, while others may not feel it is necessary for anyone to intervene, including themselves. Therefore, it is equally essential that you inquire if they would prefer you to intercede on their behalf. If the student who was gendered incorrectly conveys they desire your assistance by having you correct this inaccuracy, it is completely appropriate for this to be done. Whether this student accepts your invitation to help or not, knowing you are in their corner could have a major positive impact on the student's comfort level and well-being.

Socially transitioning can also involve other attributes which signal visual cues to allow a student to be read in a way that aligns with their affirmed gender and/or combats some aspects of gender dysphoria a student may be experiencing. For some students, wearing makeup or not wearing makeup may also be a non-invasive technique to implement and can easily be adjusted over time. There may be students who will find comfort in flattening their chest through binding, creating a flattened appearance of genitals by tucking, or constructing the visual presence of genitals by packing. In addition, some will have the need to non-surgically enhance their chest through padding, as well as padding or dressing in a manner that contours the shape of their hip area. Doing so can provide emotional relief when medical interventions are currently not an option during the transition process. Whether the student identifies as binary or non-binary, these modifications may not be visibly obvious to those working with TGNB and/or gender questioning students in school, but nevertheless, they can be occurring.

Other ways a student can socially transition is by altering their voice, mannerisms, and through movement. A person's voice is often a vital component that influences others to categorize someone's gender, and if this is improperly perceived, it can create an array of misunderstandings. Being aware of this, many TGNB students and their family members will investigate ways TGNB students can project their voice in a manner that aligns with their affirmed gender in the hope of having others, whether in person, over the school intercom, or on the phone, recognize them according to the gender with which they self-identify. A TGNB student's voice can be altered by consulting the expertise of a trans-competent, speech-language pathologist. Should this option not be accessible, those seeking this type of intervention may opt to use vocal exercises demonstrated by some online videos. There may be other manners in which students can appropriately obtain methods to alter the pitch or sound of their voice without the interventions being permanent.

People often assess a student's gender through their physical movements such as walking, dancing, sitting, lying, standing, or posing, as well as by their mannerisms and gestures. Though some TGNB and/or gender questioning students may have always conveyed physical movements, mannerisms, and gestures that match their affirmed gender, others can be consciously learning and working toward adjusting those that align with the way that they now need their gender to be viewed, while others can be completely comfortable not changing any at all. Again, regardless of the ways TGNB and/or gender questioning students visually or vocally express these characteristics, it is necessary that teachers, support staff, administrators, student peers, and others associated with the school are taught to privately ask a student what pronoun and name they use if they are uncertain. This practice is not only ideal for all TGNB and/or gender questioning students, but also for all students and adults in school settings, since it shows equal respect to everyone.

Medically transitioning is commonly what most individuals assume transitioning means, and for many, depending on their age, finances, laws, guidelines, and personal needs, this can be part of the process. Some people working in the field of education may not be aware that there are strict guidelines involving medical interventions for children and young adults. These Standards of Care (SOC), provided by the World Professional Association for Transgender Health (WPATH), are created with the utmost caution and sound medical judgment available to guide all medical and mental health professionals as to how to follow proper protocol when serving all those who identify as transgender. WPATH has specific guidelines that apply to all minors that can be accessed through its website, which is given in the resource section of this workbook. Most medical interventions are not recommended nor permitted for minors regarding any type of surgery related to gender affirmation. This is typically not a part of a minor's medical transition. Taking puberty blockers or gender-affirming hormones may be part of a student's medical transition. If either one of these interventions play a role in a student's medical transition, the student's physical development and hormone levels will be determining considerations when consulting with the child, their parents, and medical providers. Medical professionals, knowledgeable about these factors, will need to monitor Tanner stages and consult with those who are legally responsible for the student's medical decisions before deciding whether puberty blockers or gender-affirming hormones are appropriate to be used as part of their medical transition. If and when a procedure or hormone treatment is an option for a minor, based on their individual circumstances and their obtained data, important conversations will need to occur in reference to any risk factors and side effects. Detailed planning must be put in place according to WPATH guidelines and informed consent for each step has to be explained to parents and students alike. Quite often a qualified mental health professional is part of the team along with medical professionals to determine if a medical intervention is both warranted and appropriate for a minor according to SOC protocol. Being armed with the knowledge of understanding the differences between socially and medically transitioning can dispel many of the misconceptions held by those working in schools. While many TGNB students and/or those questioning their gender may socially transition in a variety of ways as minors, far fewer seem to do so medically. Nevertheless, should TGNB minors partake in medically transitioning, it is primarily hormone related.

Once transitioning aspects are understood, other aspects need to be addressed in relation to privilege and all the factors that contribute to its relevance to gender. We each bring a set of preconceived beliefs and embedded practice to each situation we encounter. Learning how to be open to broadening our core values, especially if they contradict what is being discussed, can be difficult. It is important to begin, or in some instances continue, the conversation about privilege. In our society, gendered privileges are a reality, and as students transition, these truths will most likely impact their lives, whether it is in the form of gaining or losing specific advantages they had prior to identifying on the transgender spectrum. For instance, a student who was or had the potential to be the star football player on the boys' team may no longer be entitled to play on the team or gain that college football scholarship because they are now living in their affirmed gender as female. For some non-binary students, navigating the complexities of gender binary in the world of sports is quite challenging.

There will be some well-intentioned educators who will assume particular professions or areas of interest are best suited for girls rather than boys or vice versa, causing a loss or gain of privilege by steering a student to an explicit field of study, only based on the student's accepted affirmed gender. Likewise, sometimes certain cultures and religions view a female's ability differently from a male's ability, as well as having fixed expectations of their roles in society. As a result, their family members or those close to them may have been steering their child to follow one interest or career track over the other according to their gender assigned at birth. In addition, if a TGNB and/or gender questioning student is accepted in their affirmed gender, they may no longer be permitted to participate in gender-specific traditions or customs and the reverse also holds true, both of which can possibly contribute to the loss or gain of privilege. However, once a student transitions along the binary or as non-binary, relatives and others in their life may suggest or insist on future paths they had not fostered prior to the transition, creating a loss or gain of a student's options. This is one of the many times that teachers and support staff need to expose TGNB and/or gender questioning students, regardless of gender, to the choices they have available to them that may never have been considered.

Equally important is that teachers and support staff, especially guidance counselors and social workers, must become acutely aware of and reflect on their own gender biases. More importantly, all those who teach or work with students will need to honestly assess if they have any cultural or racial biases that are gender based. Teachers, support staff, and administrators have a responsibility to engage in a truthful dialogue about the reality that patriarchy, misogyny, racism, transphobia, feminism, and male privilege exist in most school settings. These injustices not only affect TGNB and/or gender questioning students, but also the lives of all students in terms of privilege and are connected to our ability to succeed. As this is brought closer to the forefront, practices in the classroom, the manner in which a student is addressed, and the opportunities that are afforded to all students need to be revisited. In some schools, practices and policies will need to be revamped in ways that honor each person's gender identity, showing acceptance that equitable privilege is a right for all students. Furthermore, though it may be unintentional, the subtle shifts in how TGNB and/or gender questioning students are treated in terms of privilege can affect the academic, emotional, and social lives of these students. It is crucial to realize that you can be the most vital role model at this time in their life.

It cannot be overlooked that as students transition, they may be learning new social cues, perhaps investigating interests in which they were inadvertently discouraged to participate in the past. They may be struggling to comprehend all the nuances cisgender individuals have experienced since birth. Understanding the after-school clubs and activities TGNB and/or gender questioning students prefer to join, and in which participation is permitted, may be difficult for them to decipher, especially if school policies have not incorporated inclusive guidelines that welcome students as they are in transition and/or questioning their gender. By transitioning, these students can lose or gain the privilege of belonging to particular school clubs, sharing in activities like gendered dances and father-daughter/mother-son parties, or attending social events such as proms and overnight field trips. It is imperative that schools create policies that welcome TGNB and/or gender questioning students to all in-school functions and activities throughout their transition process and address all the complexities in a respectful manner while assuring their safety and well-being. It is also critical that schools review criteria as to if and why gender even needs to play a role in membership for specific clubs and events. Sometimes rules and guidelines can easily be adjusted to reflect an evolving society and recognize that, for good reason, policies change with the times. When policies are not able to be revised quickly and with ease, appropriate care and dedicated time will be required of those in power to create guidelines that guarantee the rights and privileges of TGNB and/or gender questioning students. These essential actions can enable trans-identified students to reach their full potential and gain the self-worth and confidence that will surely have a positive impact on school culture.

ANECDOTAL AFFIRMATION

ANECDOTAL AFFIRMATION

Why do YOU Need to know THAT?

This Anecdotal Affirmation is meant to inspire, provoke thought, and empower your learning in any way that opens your heart. Its presence is intended to set the tone and intention of the chapter. This affirmation may be used as a springboard for writing or as a conversation starter with someone else. Ample space has been provided for you to reflect on the Anecdotal Affirmation.

Yes, especially as a counselor, I am so used to occupying such confidential, sensitive spaces and conversations. In our training, even, disclosure is viewed as a metric of success – but for what (and whose) gain/ benefit? For what purpose or progress or protection?

GRAPHICS GALORE

Splash

Can you jot down all the words and terms that connect to the word "privilege?" As you brainstorm, write your words and terms quickly by randomly scattering them anywhere on the page in a splash-like manner. Use the information obtained from the *Splash* to assess what words and terms you already know in relation to trans vocabulary.

REFLECTIVE RESPONSES

1. What does it mean for a TGNB and/or gender questioning student to socially transition and on what information do you base this response?

. . . .

. . . .

. . . .

. . . .

. . . .

. . . .

. . . .

2. What does it mean for a TGNB and/or gender questioning student to medically transition and on what information do you base this response?

. . . .

. . . .

. . . .

. . . .

. . . .

. . . .

. . . .

3. What are some of the interventions available to TGNB and/or gender questioning students in your school in relation to socially transitioning?

....

....

....

....

....

....

....

....

4. What are some of the interventions available to TGNB and/or gender questioning students in your school in relation to medically transitioning?

....

....

....

....

....

....

....

5. Based on your own research, prior knowledge, and the information within this workbook, when applicable, with what social transition options are you comfortable having TGNB and/or gender questioning students implement and why?

....

....

....

....

....

....

....

....

6. Based on your own research, prior knowledge, and the information within this workbook, when applicable, with what social transition options are you not comfortable having TGNB and/or gender questioning students implement and why not?

....

....

....

....

....

....

....

....

7. Based on your own research, prior knowledge, and the information within this workbook, when applicable, with what medical transition options are you comfortable having TGNB and/or gender questioning students implement and why?

....

....

....

....

....

....

....

8. Based on your own research, prior knowledge, and the information within this workbook, when applicable, with what medical transition options are you not comfortable having TGNB and/or gender questioning students implement and why not?

....

....

....

....

....

....

....

9. If applicable, how were any TGNB and/or gender questioning students in your school treated by teachers, support staff, administrators, and other students, once they began to socially transition?

....

....

....

....

....

....

....

....

10. If applicable, how were any TGNB and/or gender questioning students in your school treated by teachers, support staff, administrators, and other students, once they began to medically transition?

....

....

....

....

....

....

....

11. How would you define privilege in relation to TGNB and/or gender questioning students in your classroom and/or school?

....

....

....

....

....

....

....

....

12. How do you feel privilege is affected for TGNB and/or gender questioning students in your classroom and/or school?

....

....

....

....

....

....

....

....

GAME

Matching Pre-Test 2

It is important to be aware of what you know and to use that knowledge as a starting point to grow. After taking the pre-test, you will realize what you still need to learn. The tools in this chapter were created to help you internalize the vocabulary. As a pre-test, match the vocabulary (the numbers) with the definitions (the letters) by drawing a line from a number to a letter. Each number and letter should only be used once. What were your results? The answer keys are provided in the Answer Key section in Chapter 8. It is suggested that you check your answers after you have taken the pre-test to see how well you did. Feel free to repeat this process at a later time; you may choose to use this activity to assess your progress by using this game as a post-test.

1. cisgender (cis)	A. Surgery that brings the individual's body into alignment with their gender identity.
2. cisgender privilege	B. An abbreviation that describes a person who now identifies as male gendered but was assigned a female gender at birth.
3. compersion	C. The advantages granted by society to people whose gender aligns with the gender assigned at birth.
4. deadname	D. A feeling of enjoyment while knowing your partner is experiencing joy, usually when they are romantically or sexually involved with another person. Often used as a contrast to jealousy.
5. dilate	E. A medical doctor who specializes in glands and hormones.
6. drag	F. How a person internally experiences themselves as male, female, masculine, feminine, some combination of these, or none of them; aspects of these can be culturally defined.
7. endocrinologist	G. Enacting gender for the purpose of performance or show.
8. facial feminization surgery	H. A mental health or medical professional who controls access to medical treatment such as hormones and surgery.
9. FTM/F2M/MTM/female-to-male	I. A term that describes the name assigned to a person at birth, which they no longer use, for it does not align with their affirmed gender and can also be referred to as their old name.
10. gatekeeper	J. A prescribed routine post-vaginoplasty where a person inserts medical equipment into the neovagina in order to maintain the creation of the vaginal canal.
11. gender	K. Someone whose gender assigned at birth and gender identity are aligned.
12. gender-affirming surgery (GAS)	L. A variety of plastic surgery procedures to create a more feminine appearance to the features of the face.

Retake this pre-test as a post-test to assess your personal progress and knowledge.

EMPATHY-EMBRACING EXERCISE

Gender dysphoria can motivate a student to seriously consider and eventually undergo a physical transition. If a student is feeling extremely uncomfortable with aspects of their body in relation to their gender assigned at birth, those feelings can negatively impact their socialization, the activities in which they partake, and their emotional state of mind. It can also affect their sex life in the future and current experiences. By incorporating the following exercise, teachers, support staff, and administrators have an opportunity to reflect on what makes them feel uncomfortable with their own body and have some level of understanding of the struggle a student who identifies as transgender, non-binary, and/or is questioning their gender often faces on a daily basis. While acknowledging it is not the same experience as to what a student may encounter, it is important for those who serve students in a school setting to try to understand the critical role gender dysphoria may play in a student's transition process.

Does any part of your body impede you from participating socially, affect you emotionally, or prevent you from any daily activities? Whether you answer yes or no, why do you think you feel this way? How does this make you feel? Is there any part of your body that you dislike or would prefer not to have sexually touched? Whether you answer yes or no, why do you feel this way? How does this make you feel? (It is understood that your response to this exercise may not be comfortable for you to share with anyone in a professional setting. It is important that you consider answering this privately for yourself. By doing so, you may gain more understanding of what your students who identify as transgender, non-binary, and/or are questioning their gender can experience.)

GRAPHICS GALORE

Web

There may be words or terms you do not know in relation to medically transitioning but will elect to learn more about in order to become more knowledgeable. List one new word or term in relation to medically transitioning in each outer circle that you do not know the meaning of yet or is of interest to you. Then record its definition and something novel you have acquired related to the word or term.

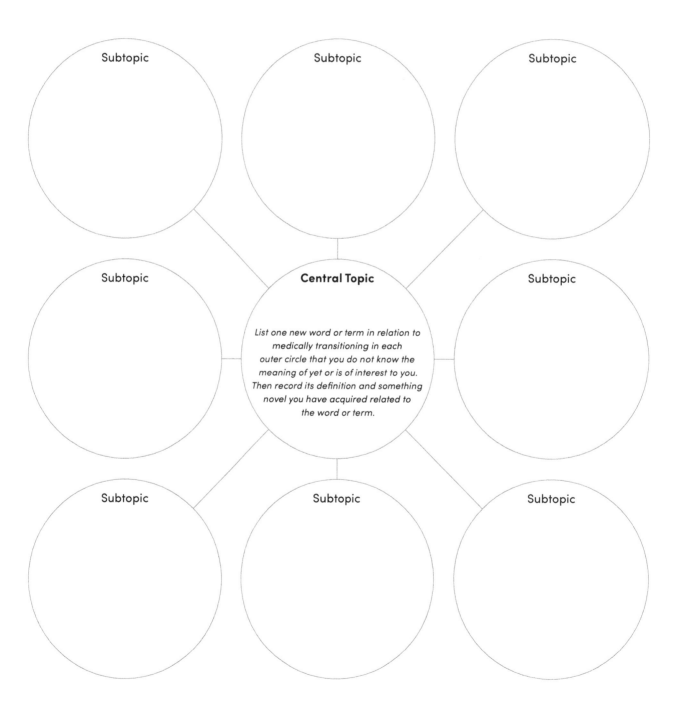

DESERVING DE-STRESSING DELIGHT

Creating or Trying Something Novel!

Learning how to incorporate much newness into one's comfort zone can cause unexpected stress for teachers, support staff, and administrators. If and when things around you feel overwhelming, building or making something that gives you a sense of strength and purpose is important. Nothing you construct needs to be earth-shattering, but each endeavor may help remind you that you have value and importance. If you love craft projects, create collages of words and pictures to express how you are feeling, knit or crochet scarves and hats, embroider or needlepoint images, and even sketch, simply to express yourself. Some people have shared that they took photographs of anything that appealed to them or designed jewelry. Others may enjoy physically building a treehouse in their backyard, painting a wall mural, carving a bed for the family pet, or studying how to sculpt bushes for their garden.

Learning something new can keep your mind sharp and busy. Try to think of a class, hobby, sport, or activity that has always interested you. Some educators and support staff may have always wanted to learn a new language, take dance lessons, or sign up for a photography course. Deep within you, you know something that has always been tucked away in the back of your mind and this is the time to clean off those cobwebs and get started. It is suggested that you base this choice on your time availability, budget constraints, and where the learning will take place in proximity to your home or work. Find whatever it is that feels creative to you and provides an outlet that validates your worthiness. Creating is an activity that can nurture and honor your talents while increasing your self-esteem and confidence level!

Journal your reaction to this Deserving De-Stressing Delight.

GAME

ABC Game

Using the vocabulary listed in the chart shown on the next page, select 12 of the words and then write each one of them on a separate index card. Mix the vocabulary word cards up and then place them in alphabetical order from left to right in a straight line. This will help you become more familiar with the vocabulary words.

VOCABULARY FOR ALL GAMES

AFAB	cisgender	gender diverse	LGBTQ/ LGBTQ+/ LGBTQQIA+	passing	TGNB
agender	cisgender privilege	gender dysphoria	metoidioplasty	phalloplasty	TGNC
AMAB	compersion	gender expression	misogyny	POC	they
androgynous	deadname	gender fluid	monogamous	polyamorous	top surgery
asexual	dilate	gender identity	MTF/FTF	preferred gender pronouns	tracheal shave
bigender	drag	gender marker	non-binary	puberty blockers	transgender/ trans-identified
bilateral mastectomy	endocrinologist	gender non-conforming	orchiectomy	queer	transitioning
binary	facial feminization surgery	genderqueer	outing	questioning	transmisogyny
binding	FTM/MTM	GnRH	packing	scrotoplasty	transphobia
bisexual	gatekeeper	GSA	pan hysterectomy	sexuality	transsexual
boi	gender	intersectionality	pansexual	stealth	two-spirit
bottom surgery	gender-affirming surgery	intersex	partner	Tanner stages	vaginoplasty

GRAPHICS GALORE

Venn Diagram

List the privileges you believe are uniquely common to cisgender boys and then uniquely common to cisgender girls. Once that is complete, list those privileges that overlap for both cisgender boys and cisgender girls. Please note that it is extremely important to acknowledge and be aware of how these perceptions of gender binary privileges affect those who identify as TGNB and/or are questioning their gender. It is equally essential for all teachers and support staff to recognize how many of these privileges can be lost or gained by a student once they identify as TGNB and/or gender questioning.

Privileges for Cisgender Boys

Privileges for Cisgender Girls

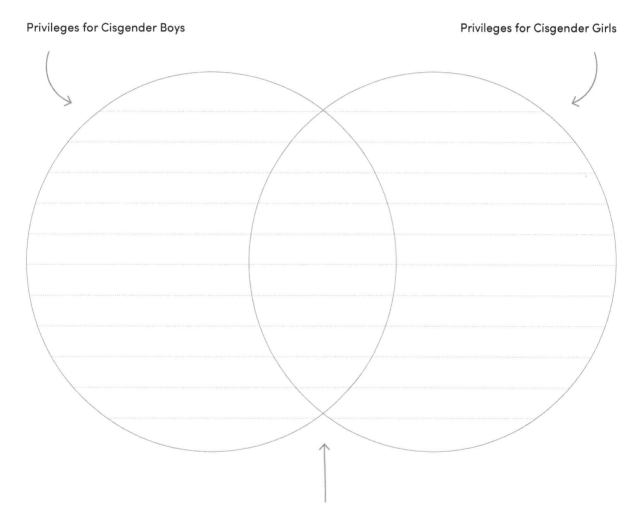

Overlapping the Privileges for Cisgender Boys
With the Privileges for Cisgender Girls

SAMPLER SHARE

I am submitting my own reply to the *Reflective Responses* question listed below as a sample, hoping to inspire you to use it as a springboard to formulate your own practices. Please be aware that all of the students' names have been removed, as well as most of the actual pronouns for the student and parent, in order to respect the privacy of TGNB and/or gender questioning students, their parents, and other family members. It should be noted that all of these methods can be beneficial for all students, not only those who identify as TGNB and/or are questioning their gender. It is imperative to understand that even without intending to, gender-based practices can negatively impact the social and emotional well-being of students who identify on the transgender spectrum. For these reasons and the need to be transparent, samples are incorporated that portray how the lives of gender-diverse students were also affected, though they did not identify themselves as TGNB and/or gender questioning at the time of the event. Whether they do now, or not, is unknown.

If applicable, how were any TGNB and/or gender questioning students in your school treated by teachers, support staff, administrators, and other students, once they began to socially transition?

One year, when I was working in an elementary school, I had a student who was questioning their gender and was slowly expressing that their identified gender was not the one they were assigned at birth. They drew themselves as their affirmed gender, much preferred to play with students who aligned with their affirmed gender, and would often put on clothing from the dress-up center without removing it until the end of the day. I worked very closely with their family to ensure the student felt comfortable within my classroom setting and I kept them informed with what I observed. We would discuss how I could support them and their child in and out of the classroom throughout the year. By the end of the year, the parents were strongly considering moving forward with gaining information in order to help their child socially transition. Since it was already late April when they made this decision, it was agreed that they would wait for this to occur at the start of the following year. However, after much research, the parent, student, their sibling, and I all decided we would attend a free, out-of-state, three-day conference during a long weekend that offered education and acceptance for families and allies of TGNB people of all ages.

For the entire three days, this student lived in an environment that enabled them to live in their affirmed gender in public and to begin to comprehend what socially transitioning could feel like in a way that validated their affirmed gender. It was a privilege to witness and I will treasure this experience for my entire life. We left the conference separately on the last day, as I knew they had plans to attend a fair close to the school. A few hours later, I received a call from the parent and I could hear my student sobbing inconsolably in the background. I could not imagine what was wrong. The parent explained that their child refused to go to the fair dressed in the clothes they would have worn in public prior to attending the conference. The panicked parent did not know what to do for they felt their child would be ridiculed by peers and their families if their child went to the fair dressed as they were at the conference. The parent asked me to talk to their child over the phone. After a lengthy conversation, a compromise was agreed upon, whereby my student would skip the fair but remain dressed in alignment with their affirmed gender until they fell asleep that evening. The parent was concerned their child would miss out if they did not attend the fair. In the end, we knew that there would be other fairs, but my student feeling like themselves for the first time in their life was much more important than anything else. After that day, there was no question in anyone's mind that this child's social transition had to be investigated and honored as soon as possible, in order for this child to be emotionally nurtured and feel whole. This student, whose social transition took two years, now lives in their affirmed gender. With one exception of conflicting bathroom-use issues that was resolved to suit my student's needs, their social transition was as seamless as one could wish. The students who were in my class with them when they first questioned their gender are still their closest friends to date. It warms my heart every time I see pictures of them all together in person and on social media!

GRAPHICS GALORE

Bar Graph

Based on a scale from 1 to 10, with 1 being the lowest and 10 being the highest, color or shade in your response. This visual will illustrate where your greatest concerns lie and can be used as a tool to help you communicate your thoughts with trainers, colleagues, administrators, parents, and students (if and when appropriate), or for your own personal understanding. The bar graph results can vary as you learn more about the Trans community, or your thinking shifts. It is critical that educators process and reflect on their feelings about the specifics of the policies that will affect the lives of students who identify as TGNB and/or gender questioning. More importantly, educators must overcome their own possible conflicting beliefs to ensure that they always treat all students with the dignity and respect they deserve.

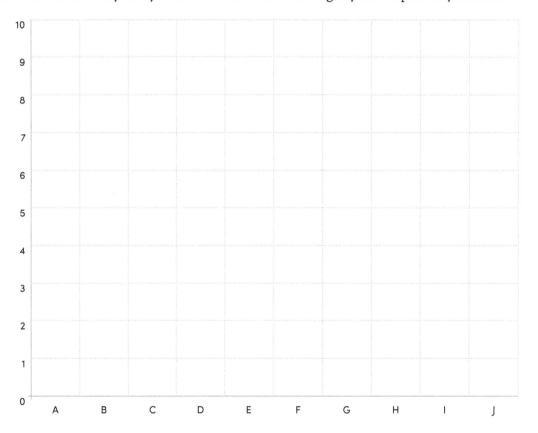

To what degree do these changes concern you as an educator in relation to the social transition of TGNB and/or gender questioning students? Your TGNB and/or gender questioning student's need to...

A. Dress in a manner that aligns with their affirmed gender.

B. Use the gender marker that aligns with their affirmed gender.

C. Be addressed by the name and/or pronoun/s that aligns with their affirmed gender.

D. Wear a wig, hair extensions, or get a haircut that aligns with their affirmed gender.

E. Speak with a more masculine or feminine voice that aligns with their affirmed gender.

F. Move their body in a manner, gesture in a way, and/or use mannerisms that align with their affirmed gender.

G. Wear makeup or not wear makeup in a manner that aligns with their affirmed gender.

H. Pad their hip area in order to align with their affirmed gender.

I. Bind or pad their chest in order to align with their affirmed gender.

J. Tuck or pack their genital area in order to align with their affirmed gender.

ANECDOTAL AFFIRMATION

This Anecdotal Affirmation is meant to inspire, provoke thought, and empower your learning in any way that opens your heart. Its presence is intended to set the tone and intention of the chapter. This affirmation may be used as a springboard for writing or as a conversation starter with someone else. Ample space has been provided for you to reflect on the Anecdotal Affirmation.

COMMUNICATION CORNER

Reflecting on your own thoughts and experiences is critical when processing new information and adjusting your thinking. Equally important can be sharing and learning how others analyze their own thoughts and experiences. This exercise was designed with the intention of offering teachers, support staff, and administrators a safe place to discuss all the topics addressed in this chapter. When two or more school employees candidly begin a conversation that embraces an open dialogue without judgment or criticism of one another's beliefs and ideas concerning students and school policies, everyone benefits. It is suggested that after teachers, support staff, and administrators privately answer the questions from the Reflective Responses section, they converse about one or two of them, while others may prefer to answer them all with a trusted colleague or administrator. In order to recall the questions you answered, simply highlight or circle the ones you addressed and then ask others the ones they responded to on their own. By doing so in a respectful and communicative manner that honors the voices of all those working or interacting with the students who identify as transgender, non-binary, and/or are questioning their gender, teachers, support staff, and administrators in your school can positively impact the lives of the students they are committed to serve as professionals. Do you and your colleague or administrator answer these questions in the same way or differently? Discuss your responses to understand how all of you view the answers to the questions and make time to celebrate all you learn from being willing to communicate with one another.

1. What does it mean for a TGNB and/or gender questioning student to socially transition and on what information do you base this response?

    . . . .

    . . . .

2. What does it mean for a TGNB and/or gender questioning student to medically transition and on what information do you base this response?

    . . . .

    . . . .

3. What are some of the interventions available to TGNB and/or gender questioning students in your school in relation to socially transitioning?

    . . . .

    . . . .

4. What are some of the interventions available to TGNB and/or gender questioning students in your school in relation to medically transitioning?

    . . . .

    . . . .

5. Based on your own research, prior knowledge, and the information within this workbook, when applicable, with what social transition options are you comfortable having TGNB and/or gender questioning students implement and why?

    . . . .

    . . . .

6. Based on your own research, prior knowledge, and the information within this workbook, when applicable, with what social transition options are you not comfortable having TGNB and/or gender questioning students implement and why not?

    . . . .

    . . . .

7. Based on your own research, prior knowledge, and the information within this workbook, when applicable, with what medical transition options are you comfortable having TGNB and/or gender questioning students implement and why?

    . . . .

    . . . .

8. Based on your own research, prior knowledge, and the information within this workbook, when applicable, with what medical transition options are you not comfortable having TGNB and/or gender questioning students implement and why not?

. . . .

. . . .

9. If applicable, how were any TGNB and/or gender questioning students in your school treated by teachers, support staff, administrators, and other students, once they began to socially transition?

. . . .

. . . .

10. If applicable, how were any TGNB and/or gender questioning students in your school treated by teachers, support staff, administrators, and other students, once they began to medically transition?

. . . .

. . . .

11. How would you define privilege in relation to TGNB and/or gender questioning students in your classroom and/or school?

. . . .

. . . .

12. How do you feel privilege is affected for TGNB and/or gender questioning students in your classroom and/or school?

. . . .

. . . .

Chapter 4

TALKING TO PARENTS AND STUDENTS

VITAL VIGNETTE

Regardless of their level of acceptance, as their child begins to transition and/or questions their gender, family members are sometimes overwhelmed with concerns, questions, and unknowns. Foremost on their mind is wondering how life will be for their child at school. Will their child have friends? Will their child be safe at school? Who will protect their child when they are not there? What school policies are currently part of school guidelines to ensure the needs of their child? Can their child still participate in the same clubs and activities they did before this process began? Which school bathroom will their child use and what are their rights in relation to this decision? How can they be assured their child will be referred to by their affirmed name and pronoun? Will they, as parents and other family members, be blamed, shamed, or judged poorly by school personnel? How much of an advocate will each parent need to be for their child? How will the transition affect the school life of the other children in their family? Who creates the school policies that will affect their child's school days? Will their child be able to learn and remain under the care of those at school? Should they inform the school that their child is transitioning and/or questioning their gender? What are the first steps when speaking to school personnel about their child's transition and/or gender questioning? Is their family the first family in the district to have a child identify as TGNB and/or gender questioning? The list of concerns, questions, and unknowns is endless and constantly changing.

These ambivalences can be extremely similar for many educators as they learn that their students may be transitioning and/or questioning their gender. The angst may not be completely the same but the inquiries are often quite aligned. Knowledge is power, as many have heard time and time again, for when schools transition as their students transition, there can be no truer statement. It is critical for all those who work in a school to be trained and to have the policies, procedures, and rights of their TGNB and/or gender questioning students explained. Furthermore, all laws applicable to TGNB students must be investigated, understood, and followed to the letter. School policies will need to be established quickly and when possible, created prior to learning that a student in the school identifies as TGNB and/or is questioning their gender. Recognizing that TGNB students are or will be transitioning while under the care of schools should alert schools that time is of the essence. This is reason enough for school policy makers to be proactive and research the law as they learn about the rights of TGNB and/or gender questioning students.

Though teachers, support staff, and administrators may have close bonds with families and students and can often feel comfortable discussing a variety of topics with each other, talking about transitioning may be more challenging. When it is appropriate to begin the conversation, many schools can look to social workers, school nurses, guidance counselors, and school psychologists to be the leaders on TGNB protocol. Quite often, this is because they are usually more familiar with approaching highly personal and private issues with families as part of their professional training. If not currently experienced in working with the Trans community, these skilled personnel will need to educate themselves on the specific issues, concerns, and obstacles TGNB students and their families can face on a daily basis.

It is crucial to understand that if a mental health or medical professional is experienced with gay, lesbian, and bisexual (LGB) issues and topics, this does not necessarily qualify them to help students who identify as TGNB or those in the Trans (T) community. This simply means they need to have adequate training to properly serve the trans population in their school, for "LGB" refers to sexuality and "T" refers to gender, with each group having their own separate needs and protocol. Though there can be some overlapping and interrelated issues, mental and medical health professionals, as well as all those creating school policies in connection to TGNB and/or gender questioning students, must be aware of and prepared to address the multiple and vital differences between the two. Some schools may prefer their social workers, school nurses, guidance counselors, and school psychologists to train staff members about relevant trans-related matters. However, other schools may elect to create a team that incorporates some of them but is further broadened by classroom teachers, support staff, families, students, and community members.

Asking TGNB students and their families questions that will affect their lives, as well as including them in the formation of school policies, can be one of the most honorable ways a school can show a level of respect for their needs. It is imperative to inquire what issues are priorities to ensure their child and other TGNB and/or gender questioning students' needs are met. Likewise, it is key to request their input when formulating school policies and to check how family members want the outcomes to be reviewed with them. It is essential to speak with families about what they want or need regarding their level of involvement in their own training or in training others. Moreover, it is necessary to inquire exactly what is acceptable for school personnel to share with whom and when. The above actions are thoughtful and dignified practices that schools should adopt to support all involved. Every school will need to figure out what works best for their circumstances. In addition, all laws must be honored and the utmost focus must be the welfare and well-being of the TGNB students and their families.

It is crucial that whoever a school assigns to work with TGNB students and their families recognizes that quite often students opt to remain private about their need to transition and/or question their gender because they fear they will burden, alienate, or embarrass their family. Some students will silently suffer and sacrifice what will enable them to feel whole to spare any anticipated and/or concerning challenges that may lie ahead for them and their families. In fact, many students, even young children, will not have the words or mature language to express all they are feeling and experiencing within themselves and can be internally conflicted in regard to exposing their emotional turmoil. As a result, these students may become or feel socially isolated, begin to regress and struggle academically, act out inappropriately, and tragically contemplate suicide. Whereas, family members can be grappling with suspecting or realizing that their child needs to transition and/or that their child is questioning their gender without knowing who to turn to for advice and help. They, too, may be experiencing a wide array of emotions and fears, sometimes feeling lost and alone. Even those family members who are active advocates for their child can need support and additional guidance. It is incumbent on schools to employ trained professionals who will support this process for TGNB and/or gender questioning students by providing a referral list of qualified outside mental and medical health professionals, clinics, and support group information for TGNB students and their families, especially if a school cannot offer these vital services.

As with all new policy decisions and the introduction of topics of which the general school community may not be aware, similar concerns, questions, and unknowns that were posed at the top of the chapter will also be meaningful to them. Teachers and support staff, as well as all other school personnel, will need to be guided as to how to appropriately answer inquiries posed by community members, the parents of non-TGNB students, the family members of TGNB students, and students in their school. Understanding how they will be informed of current school policies and protocol, what information school personnel are legally permitted to share about a TGNB student's gender, and with whom they could question and confer should they themselves require more clarification, will need to be addressed. Providing up-to-date sources that include appropriate conferences, experienced speakers, and knowledgeable trainers who are in the Trans community, or are respected in the Trans community, will be essential. Offering training led by well-informed school mental health professionals and school counselors on trans topics, as well as experts in the field of trans issues, has to be part of the resource package. These individuals will need to present opportunities for students and school personnel alike to ask questions, vent concerns, and learn about all the unknowns. In addition, it is important to make available reading materials in the form of current books and workbooks to enhance supplementary learning for school personnel, families, and students. Furthermore, credible online websites, vetted online groups, and podcasts are also key ways for those who prefer and seek this type of format to gather research and process new information. Lastly, inviting TGNB community members to speak about their personal experiences and TGNB professionals to answer policy and legal questions posed by school personnel and students can afford TGNB and/or gender questioning students the opportunity to meet role models from the Trans community.

Honoring the wishes of students and their families should be handled with compassion, always showing sensitivity while preserving the dignity of all involved. Some families may prefer not to share their knowledge of the transition with school officials, though their child might feel differently. Other families may opt to wait to tell others until all school policies are in place. Still other families will support their child's urgent need to live in their affirmed gender immediately, before school policies are in play. This may be the result of families recognizing the emotional toll it can take on their child if they are forced to postpone aspects of the transition. Moreover, allowances must be made and understood as TGNB and/or gender questioning students and their family members reserve the right to alter the decisions they may have previously chosen, regardless of their reasons. Providing the necessary time and available options to students and their family members as they make the difficult choices as to when, how, if, and why to disclose information about the transition is critical. Offering respectful guidance and information pertaining to current school-related policies and protocol can greatly assist them when they are faced with important determinations that will impact the life of their child and other family members. Whether families decide to disclose or not and/or are all in agreement, step-by-step plans will still require their input and expressed wishes. Regardless of their decision, TGNB and/or gender questioning students' education, emotional welfare, safety, and inclusion in school-life activities will need to be paramount.

Protocol cannot be based on the objections of others, for the challenges will demand their own form of education without damaging the well-being of the TGNB student. Schools should be prepared for oppositional and supportive sectors, but deliberately choose to build on the latter as a viable group to move appropriate and honorable policies forward. Quite often, once legal rulings are explained and misconceptions are debunked, community members will be able to work through their own fears and in turn, become vociferous advocates of trans rights in schools. This will enable TGNB and/or gender questioning students to be seen in a positive light and feel equally protected by those who may not have considered being proactive prior to their new awareness. For those who continue to be resistant, as in other circumstances, it is still necessary for them to cause no harm and be held accountable if they do so. This must also be true for any school personnel who do not abide by the law, school policies, and the rights of families, once the school mutually agrees to specific guidelines and procedures. Training the entire school and educating the general public are mammoth tasks, but not assuming this responsibility is unacceptable and most importantly, will greatly contribute to causing undeserving harm to TGNB and/or gender questioning students while attending school.

ANECDOTAL AFFIRMATION

ANECDOTAL AFFIRMATION

When I am not there,
Will you live in fear?
Please let those
At school,
Be fair and care!

This Anecdotal Affirmation is meant to inspire, provoke thought, and empower your learning in any way that opens your heart. Its presence is intended to set the tone and intention of the chapter. This affirmation may be used as a springboard for writing or as a conversation starter with someone else. Ample space has been provided for you to reflect on the Anecdotal Affirmation.

....

....

....

....

....

....

....

....

....

....

....

....

....

....

....

GRAPHICS GALORE

Splash

Can you jot down all of the types of resources that are or should be available to school personnel, parents, and students in regard to supporting the needs of TGNB and/or gender questioning students in your school? As you brainstorm, write the types of resources quickly by randomly scattering them anywhere on the page in a splash-like manner. Use the information obtained from the *Splash* to assess what types of resources you already have in relation to trans resources.

REFLECTIVE RESPONSES

1. What topics and inquiries about which you are knowledgeable do you feel comfortable discussing with parents, guardians, caregivers, and other family members in relation to trans issues, on your own or in the presence of another professional?

    . . . .

    . . . .

    . . . .

    . . . .

    . . . .

    . . . .

    . . . .

    . . . .

2. What topics and inquiries about which you are knowledgeable do you feel comfortable discussing with TGNB and/or gender questioning students in relation to trans issues, on your own or in the presence of another professional?

    . . . .

    . . . .

    . . . .

    . . . .

    . . . .

    . . . .

    . . . .

3. What are your school's current policies, guidelines, and procedures in relation to gender stereotypes that not only affect the lives of TGNB and/or gender questioning students, but also the lives of cisgender students in your classroom and/or school?

....

....

....

....

....

....

....

4. What are your school's current policies, guidelines, and procedures in relation to the needs and safety of TGNB and/or gender questioning students in your classroom and/or school?

....

....

....

....

....

....

....

5. How will or does your school convey the current policies, guidelines, and procedures
    to teachers, support staff, and other personnel in relation to the needs and safety of
    TGNB and/or gender questioning students in your classroom and/or school?

    . . . .

    . . . .

    . . . .

    . . . .

    . . . .

    . . . .

    . . . .

    . . . .

6. How will or does your school convey the current policies, guidelines, and procedures to
    all parents, guardians, caregivers, and other family members in relation to the needs and
    safety of TGNB and/or gender questioning students in your classroom and/or school?

    . . . .

    . . . .

    . . . .

    . . . .

    . . . .

    . . . .

    . . . .

7. How will or does your school convey the current policies, guidelines, and procedures for implementation to all students in relation to the needs and safety of TGNB and/or gender questioning students in your classroom and/or school?

. . . .

. . . .

. . . .

. . . .

. . . .

. . . .

. . . .

8. What type of training and follow-up will be provided for teachers, support staff, and other personnel in relation to the needs and safety of TGNB and/or gender questioning students in your classroom and/or school?

. . . .

. . . .

. . . .

. . . .

. . . .

. . . .

. . . .

9. What type of training and follow-up will be provided for the entire student body in relation to the needs and safety of TGNB and/or gender questioning students in your classroom and/or school?

....

....

....

....

....

....

....

....

10. What are the by-laws in your school's jurisdiction that must be honored and accepted in relation to the needs and safety of TGNB and/or gender questioning students in your classroom and/or school?

....

....

....

....

....

....

....

....

11. How and by whom will the by-laws in your school's jurisdiction be introduced, implemented, and continuously updated for all school personnel, parents, and students in relation to the needs and safety of TGNB and/or gender questioning students in your school and/or classroom?

....

....

....

....

....

....

....

....

12. How will your school incorporate and support counseling, in and out of school, for TGNB and/or gender questioning students and their families, as well as resources and information for those who request these services and assistance?

....

....

....

....

....

....

....

GAME

Matching Pre-Test 3

It is important to be aware of what you know and to use that knowledge as a starting point to grow. After taking the pre-test, you will realize what you still need to learn. The tools in this chapter were created to help you internalize the vocabulary. As a pre-test, match the vocabulary (the numbers) with the definitions (the letters) by drawing a line from a number to a letter. Each number and letter should only be used once. What were your results? The answer keys are provided in the Answer Key section in Chapter 8. It is suggested that you check your answers after you have taken the pre-test to see how well you did. Feel free to repeat this process at a later time; you may choose to use this activity to assess your progress by using this game as a post-test.

1. gender diverse	A. A term for people who do not meet common gender norms.
2. gender dysphoria	B. A medical term for the hormone that is released by the hypothalamus governing the production of LH (Luteinizing Hormone) and FSH (Follicle-Stimulating Hormone) by the pituitary gland, which causes the gonads to produce estrogen and testosterone.
3. gender expression	C. One's internal sense of being masculine-identified, feminine-identified, neither, or both.
4. gender fluid	D. The uncomfortable, distressing, anxiety-provoking, and/or sometimes depressing feelings that occur in people when aspects of their body and behavior are not congruent with their gender identity.
5. gender identity	E. The manner in which a person demonstrates their masculinity and/or femininity that can include clothing, body, behavior, speech, gestures, and other forms of appearance.
6. gender marker	F. A term that recognizes individuals whose gender may not be viewed by others and/or themselves as aligning with cultural norms based on their gender expression, identity, and/or role in society.
7. gender non-conforming	G. A gender identity and expression that encompasses a variety of aspects related to femininity and masculinity that could change over time.
8. genderqueer	H. The legal designation of one's gender on official documentation or records.
9. GnRH (Gonadotropin Releasing Hormone)	I. A group of medical conditions where someone can be born with ambiguous genitalia and/or internal sex organs or chromosomal differences that are not clearly male or female.
10. GSA	J. The lens through which one should look at all the multiple identities involved in their or others' lived experience.
11. intersectionality	K. An abbreviation that stands for Gender and Sexualities Alliance, Gay-Straight Alliance, or Gender and Sexuality Alliance and is a school club for students to meet, organize, and educate around issues pertaining to gender and sexuality.
12. intersex	L. A gender that is not exclusively masculine or exclusively feminine and is outside the gender binary.

Retake this pre-test as a post-test to assess your personal progress and knowledge.

EMPATHY-EMBRACING EXERCISE

Understanding the need a student has to transition can sometimes be a challenge for teachers, support staff, and administrators. Trying to view the process through the student's lens may be an important step towards acceptance. Sometimes the safest and most comfortable place to discuss and sort out all of these feelings is with a counselor, a support group, by attending a conference, or from searching the internet.

How do you think it would feel if you were asked to not live in your affirmed gender?

GRAPHICS GALORE

Web

Knowing those in charge of creating policies and guidelines can be extremely helpful when teachers, support staff, parents, and students need them altered or instituted. List the contact information for individuals and organizations that make the decisions affecting TGNB and/or gender questioning students in school. This can prove to be very useful for future use when it may become necessary to advocate for these students. This graphic organizer provides a structured space for you to record this data in one location and add to the list as you gain more information. Record their name, pronoun, job title/position, how you know of them, and their email and phone number.

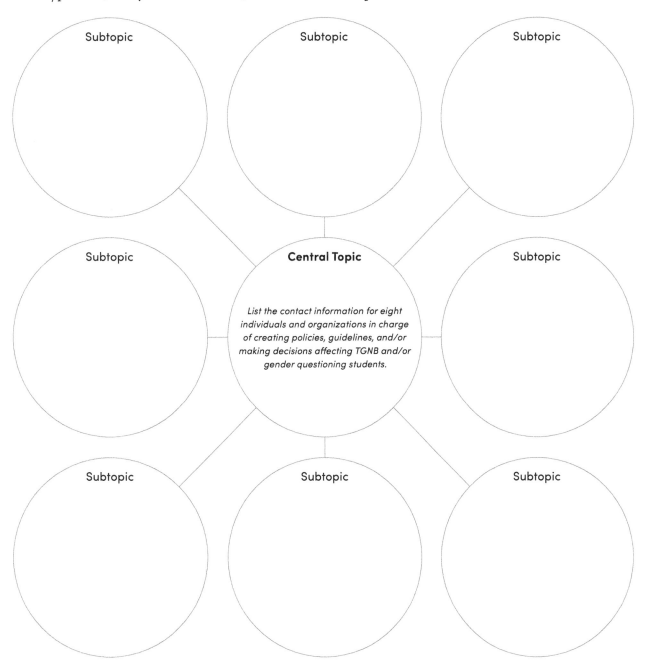

DESERVING DE-STRESSING DELIGHT

Time with Family Members and Friends

It is critical to nurture your relationships with family members and friends. Sometimes work can be all-consuming and spending time with those you love and care about can take a back seat to your career or mandatory deadlines. One healthy way to address this is to schedule time with family members and friends, where the focus is on joining them for outings, activities, and events that they express are important. Some days this will be extremely difficult to do, but those are probably the days that these relationships will need it the most.

Plan how the structured time can be scheduled. Some teachers and support staff select one day or evening a week to do something their entire family enjoys as a unit. Others attend a get-away trip with friends. Still others alternate having family members plan their time together. This can be a one-to-one scheduled time with a particular family member or close friend, if that is preferred. You may want to discuss these ideas when negotiating the ground rules in relation to this quality time together.

Questions you may ask one another include:

· Which family members and friends will be included?
· What type of things do you still like to do together?
· What will be the budget?
· Who will plan this time?
· How often will this occur?
· How will this be scheduled?

Whether family members and friends elect to participate or not, it is suggested that you continue carving out time for those who mean a great deal to you by intentionally creating the space to build memories and experiences. Even as the work commitments pile up, try not to allow these pressures to interfere with the relationships that mean the most to you!

Journal your reaction to this Deserving De-Stressing Delight.

. . . .

. . . .

. . . .

. . . .

. . . .

GAME

Mix-n-Match

Print a copy of all the vocabulary words and definition cards provided on the following pages, then cut up and glue/tape all of the words and the definitions from the vocabulary cards onto index cards. Next, select the 12 words and their matching meanings from any one of the Pre-Tests and use the index cards they are on to play the *Mix-n-Match* game.

Randomly place the 12 vocabulary word cards face down, on the left side of a flat surface, in a vertical line from top to bottom. Then player one randomly places the 12 vocabulary definition cards face down, on the right side of the same flat surface, in a 3x4 configuration that is visually three rows of four cards. Now, player one turns over the top card from the vertical line of vocabulary word cards and reads it aloud. Finally, the same player turns over any one of the vocabulary definition cards from the 3x4 configuration and reads it aloud. If they match, then player one keeps the matching pair and turns over the next vocabulary word card from the top of the vertical line and goes again by repeating the same directions. If they do not match, player one turns the vocabulary definition card back over, but keeps the vocabulary word card face up on the top of the vertical line. The next player turns a new vocabulary definition card over and reads both the vocabulary word card and new vocabulary definition card aloud. If they match, then player two keeps the matching pair and turns over the next vocabulary word card from the top of the vertical line and goes again by repeating the same directions. If the cards do not match, player two turns the vocabulary definition card back over, but keeps the vocabulary word card face up on the vertical line. This process continues for all players, as long as necessary, until all pairs are matched. The player with the most pairs wins the game.

An alternative is to play this game with the vocabulary definition cards forming the vertical line, from top to bottom, on the left side of a flat surface and the vocabulary word cards forming the 3x4 configuration on the right side of the same flat surface. You may elect to play with only the vocabulary words or only the definitions you do not know, in order to master them, or use any combination of words and definitions provided below.

AFAB	An abbreviation that stands for an individual who was assigned female at birth by a medical doctor based on the visible appearance of their genitalia at birth.	agender	Someone who does not identify with any gender.
AMAB	An abbreviation that stands for an individual who was assigned male at birth by a medical doctor based on the visible appearance of their genitalia at birth.	androgynous	Someone who possesses both masculine and feminine characteristics.
asexual	Someone who does not feel sexual attraction to other people.	bigender	Someone who experiences themselves as both masculine and feminine.
bilateral mastectomy	A surgical procedure that removes breast tissue from both sides of the chest and can include the construction of a male-appearing chest.	binary	The belief that there are only two genders: male and female.

binding	*A practice of using material or clothing to constrict the breasts that enables a person to flatten their chest.*	bisexual (bi)	*A person who is attracted to both masculine and feminine people.*
boi	*It can designate a number of sexual orientations and possibilities that are not mutually exclusive and may also refer to someone assigned female at birth but who does not identify as, or only partially identifies as, a girl or woman; moreover, they often identify as lesbians, dykes, or queer.*	bottom surgery	*A surgical procedure that permanently changes the genitals or internal reproductive organs.*
cisgender (cis)	*Someone whose gender assigned at birth and gender identity are aligned.*	cisgender privilege	*The advantages granted by society to people whose gender aligns with the gender assigned at birth.*
compersion	*A feeling of enjoyment while knowing your partner is experiencing joy, usually when they are romantically or sexually involved with another person. Often used as a contrast to jealousy.*	deadname	*A term that describes the name assigned to a person at birth, which they no longer use, for it does not align with their affirmed gender and can also be referred to as their old name.*

dilate	A prescribed routine post-vaginoplasty where a person inserts medical equipment into the neovagina in order to maintain the creation of the vaginal canal.	drag	Enacting gender for the purpose of performance or show.
endocrinologist	A medical doctor who specializes in glands and hormones.	facial feminization surgery	A variety of plastic surgery procedures to create a more feminine appearance to the features of the face.
FTM (used in games) F-T-M female-to-male F2M MTM M-T-M	An abbreviation that describes a person who now identifies as male gendered but was assigned a female gender at birth.	gatekeeper	A mental health or medical professional who controls access to medical treatment such as hormones and surgery.
gender	How a person internally experiences themselves as male, female, masculine, feminine, some combination of these, or none of them; aspects of these can be culturally defined.	gender-affirming surgery (GAS)	Surgery that brings the individual's body into alignment with their gender identity.

gender diverse	A term that recognizes individuals whose gender may not be viewed by others and/or themselves as aligning with cultural norms based on their gender expression, identity, and/or role in society.	gender dysphoria	The uncomfortable, distressing, anxiety-provoking, and/or sometimes depressing feelings that occur in people when aspects of their body and behavior are not congruent with their gender identity.
gender expression	The manner in which a person demonstrates their masculinity and/or femininity that can include clothing, body, behavior, speech, gestures, and other forms of appearance.	gender fluid	A gender identity and expression that encompasses a variety of aspects related to femininity and masculinity that could change over time.
gender identity	One's internal sense of being masculine-identified, feminine-identified, neither, or both.	gender marker	The legal designation of one's gender on official documentation or records.
gender non-conforming	A term for people who do not meet common gender norms.	genderqueer	A gender that is not exclusively masculine or exclusively feminine and is outside the gender binary.

GnRH (Gonadotropin Releasing Hormone)	A medical term for the hormone that is released by the hypothalamus governing the production of LH and FSH by the pituitary gland, which causes the gonads to produce estrogen and testosterone.	GSA	An abbreviation that stands for Gender and Sexualities Alliance, Gay-Straight Alliance, or Gender and Sexuality Alliance and is a school club for students to meet, organize, and educate around issues pertaining to gender and sexuality.
intersectionality	The lens through which one should look at all the multiple identities involved in their or others' lived experience.	intersex	A group of medical conditions where someone can be born with ambiguous genitalia and/or internal sex organs or chromosomal differences that are not clearly male or female.
LGBTQ LGBTQ+ LGBTQQIA+ (definition matches this abbreviation)	An all-encompassing abbreviation which stands for lesbian, gay, bisexual, transgender, queer, questioning, intersex, allies, plus others.	metoidioplasty	A gender-affirming bottom surgery which releases the micro phallus and can include urethra lengthening.
misogyny	A disdain, hatred, or mistrust of all people female and feminine.	monogamous	A type of relationship where a person is sexually and/or romantically involved with only one person at a time.

MTF (used in games) M-T-F male-to-female M2F FTF F-T-F	An abbreviation that describes a person who now identifies as female gendered but was assigned a male gender at birth.	non-binary	A gender that is not exclusively male or exclusively female and is outside the gender binary.
orchiectomy	A type of bottom surgery that involves the removal of testicles.	outing	The act of disclosing someone's sexuality and/or gender identity without their knowledge and/or permission.
packing	The use of prosthetics and other materials to enable an individual to possess the appearance and feeling of having a penis and testicles.	pan hysterectomy	A type of bottom surgery that usually includes removing the uterus, ovaries, and fallopian tubes and which could involve the removal of the cervix.
pansexual	Someone who is attracted to people of various genders.	partner	A person who is in a sexual and/or romantic relationship with someone.

passing	The ability for a person to be read as their affirmed gender by those who are unaware that the individual's identity is transgender.	phalloplasty	A type of bottom surgery that entails the construction of a penis and can include the construction of testicles and the implant of an erection device.
POC	An abbreviation that stands for a Person/People of Color.	polyamorous	A type of relationship where a person is sexually and/or romantically involved with more than one person at the same time.
preferred gender pronouns (PGP)	The practice of using or referring to a person in the way an individual needs to be addressed, also known as proper gender pronouns.	puberty blockers	A term for a medicine that blocks the hormone GnRH (Gonadotropin Releasing Hormone).
queer	A word that refers to a sexual orientation that is not heterosexual and/or anything that is non-heteronormative.	questioning	The act of a person who is attempting to figure out their own sexuality and/or gender.

scrotoplasty	A surgical procedure that creates a scrotal sac and can include testicular implants.	sexuality	The pattern of thoughts, feelings, and arousal that determine sexual preferences.
stealth	A word used for a transgender person who chooses to keep their trans status private.	Tanner stages	A system to classify the development of puberty in children.
TGNB	An abbreviation that stands for Transgender and Non-Binary or Transgender and Gender Non-Binary, also described as Transgender/Non-Binary.	TGNC	An abbreviation that stands for Transgender and Gender Non-Conforming, also described as Transgender/Gender Non-Conforming.
they	A word that may be used as a gender-neutral pronoun to describe a single individual.	top surgery	A surgical procedure made to create a masculine-appearing chest or to have breast implants.

tracheal shave	A surgical procedure that reduces the thyroid cartilage, which makes up the Adam's apple.	trans	An inclusive umbrella word for all those who identify on the transgender spectrum.
transgender/ trans-identified	An overarching word which can be used for people whose gender expression and/or gender identity does not align with their sex assigned at birth.	transitioning	The social and/or medical actions a person takes to explore and/or affirm their gender identity.
transmisogyny	A word coined by Julia Serano to describe a form of misogyny that is focused towards trans women.	transphobia	Prejudice, fear, disdain, or discrimination in respect to gender non-conforming and transgender people.
transsexual	A person who identifies within the gender binary (either male or female) and may have medical procedures to bring their body in line with their identity. However, not all transgender people who have medical transitions identify as this word.	two-spirit	An Indigenous North American identity embraced by some individuals who incorporate a variety of gender roles, identities, and expressions by embodying both masculine and feminine spirits and traits.

vaginoplasty	*The surgical construction of a vagina.*		

GRAPHICS GALORE

T-Chart

Write down what specific policies and procedures parents and/or TGNB students **"Know"** your school has in place in relation to addressing the needs of TGNB and/or gender questioning students, what specific policies and procedures do parents and/or TGNB students **"Want"** to be in place in relation to addressing the needs of TGNB and/or gender questioning students, and what specific policies and procedures have parents and/or TGNB students **"Learned"** are necessary to be in place in relation to addressing the needs of TGNB and/or gender questioning students, regarding the safety and welfare of these students in your school.

Topic	Know	Want	Learned
1.			
2.			
3.			
4.			
5.			
6.			
7.			

SAMPLER SHARE

I am submitting my own reply to the Reflective Responses question listed below as a sample, hoping to inspire you to use it as a springboard to formulate your own practices. Please be aware that all of the students' names have been removed, as well as most of the actual pronouns for the student and parent, in order to respect the privacy of TGNB and/or gender questioning students, their parents, and other family members. It should be noted that all of these methods can be beneficial for all students, not only those who identify as TGNB and/or are questioning their gender. It is imperative to understand that even without intending to, gender-based practices can negatively impact the social and emotional well-being of students who identify on the transgender spectrum. For these reasons and the need to be transparent, samples are incorporated that portray how the lives of gender-diverse students were also affected, though they did not identify themselves as TGNB and/or gender questioning at the time of the event. Whether they do now, or not, is unknown.

What are your school's current policies, guidelines, and procedures in relation to gender stereotypes that not only affect the lives of TGNB and/or gender questioning students, but also the lives of cisgender students in your classroom and/or school?

For many years, I would spend my winter break in New Orleans and always returned to school with dozens of strands of beads I caught from the float celebrations. As a Valentine's Day gift to the students, I would spill out a large array of necklaces onto my carpet and the sounds of glee and excitement from the students would fill my heart. Prior to the distribution of the gift, we discussed the importance of supporting a person's necklace preference and that whatever a student chose was to be acceptable to everyone. To be true to my philosophy of offering the same options to all students, regardless of their gender identity, I would pull the students' names out of a bag and one by one they would select the necklace that they liked. As always, one of the most popular versions was the "pearl" necklace. I recall one of my students picking this one in particular and he joyfully wore it all day long. Being who I was as a teacher, I supported his choice but was unsure of how his parents would respond if he brought it home. I was well aware that all the parents were clear as to my beliefs as an educator, and so, as with all the other students, he wore his home. One of his parents showed up outside my classroom the next day with the necklace in their hand. I remember being worried what this parent was going to say or do. Just as I began to explain that this was their child's choice and that I felt their child had every right to select the necklace based on a policy I explained at Meet-the-Teacher Night, the parent interrupted my defense. The parent stated that they agreed with the policy and that they were not surprised that their son selected this necklace. In fact, they had no problem with their son's choice at all. The parent continued that they loved their child and wanted my guarantee that I would protect their child from being bullied or harmed at school for wearing the "pearl" necklace.

Whether this student would eventually identify as TGNB or not did not matter. What did matter was that my role as a teacher was not only to educate this child academically but also to provide a safe space for him to be true to himself. He wore that beaded "pearl" necklace for many weeks and his classmates were always in his corner. What this experience reinforced was that I had to continue to be a vocal advocate for all students, regardless of the gender with which they identified. In addition, it became increasingly clear that it was also my responsibility to safeguard policies that ensured every student had the freedom to feel comfortable with their gender expression in all school settings.

GRAPHICS GALORE

Box

List all the different groups of people who have contact with students throughout the school year. The purpose of this graphic organizer is to become aware of all the individuals who must be appropriately trained on how to support and respect TGNB and/or gender questioning students in your school. This data should include, but is not limited to, those that apply to your school: teachers, support staff, substitutes, parents, students, secretaries, custodians, nurses, counselors, bus drivers, greeters, aides, administrators, student teachers, cafeteria staff, parent-teacher association members, security guards, volunteers, special area teachers, and board members.

1	2	3	4	5
6	7	8	9	10
11	12	13	14	15
16	17	18	19	20
21	22	23	24	25

ANECDOTAL AFFIRMATION

ANECDOTAL AFFIRMATION

*My child's safety
In school,
Needs to be
The golden rule!*

This Anecdotal Affirmation is meant to inspire, provoke thought, and empower your learning in any way that opens your heart. Its presence is intended to set the tone and intention of the chapter. This affirmation may be used as a springboard for writing or as a conversation starter with someone else. Ample space has been provided for you to reflect on the Anecdotal Affirmation.

COMMUNICATION CORNER

Reflecting on your own thoughts and experiences is critical when processing new information and adjusting your thinking. Equally important can be sharing and learning how others analyze their own thoughts and experiences. This exercise was designed with the intention of offering teachers, support staff, and administrators a safe place to discuss all the topics addressed in this chapter. When two or more school employees candidly begin a conversation that embraces an open dialogue without judgment or criticism of one another's beliefs and ideas concerning students and school policies, everyone benefits. It is suggested that after teachers, support staff, and administrators privately answer the questions from the Reflective Responses section, they converse about one or two of them, while others may prefer to answer them all with a trusted colleague or administrator. In order to recall the questions you answered, simply highlight or circle the ones you addressed and then ask others the ones they responded to on their own. By doing so in a respectful and communicative manner that honors the voices of all those working or interacting with the students who identify as transgender, non-binary, and/or are questioning their gender, teachers, support staff, and administrators in your school can positively impact the lives of the students they are committed to serve as professionals. Do you and your colleague or administrator answer these questions in the same way or differently? Discuss your responses to understand how all of you view the answers to the questions and make time to celebrate all you learn from being willing to communicate with one another.

1. What topics and inquiries about which you are knowledgeable do you feel comfortable discussing with parents, guardians, caregivers, and other family members in relation to trans issues, on your own or in the presence of another professional?

   . . . .

   . . . .

2. What topics and inquiries about which you are knowledgeable do you feel comfortable discussing with TGNB and/or gender questioning students in relation to trans issues, on your own or in the presence of another professional?

   . . . .

   . . . .

3. What are your school's current policies, guidelines, and procedures in relation to gender stereotypes that not only affect the lives of TGNB and/or gender questioning students, but also the lives of cisgender students in your classroom and/or school?

    . . . .

    . . . .

4. What are your school's current policies, guidelines, and procedures in relation to the needs and safety of TGNB and/or gender questioning students in your classroom and/or school?

    . . . .

    . . . .

5. How will or does your school convey the current policies, guidelines, and procedures to teachers, support staff, and other personnel in relation to the needs and safety of TGNB and/or gender questioning students in your classroom and/or school?

    . . . .

    . . . .

6. How will or does your school convey the current policies, guidelines, and procedures to all parents, guardians, caregivers, and other family members in relation to the needs and safety of TGNB and/or gender questioning students in your classroom and/or school?

    . . . .

    . . . .

7. How will or does your school convey the current policies, guidelines, and procedures for implementation to all students in relation to the needs and safety of TGNB and/or gender questioning students in your classroom and/or school?

    . . . .

    . . . .

8. What type of training and follow-up will be provided for teachers, support staff, and other personnel in relation to the needs and safety of TGNB and/ or gender questioning students in your classroom and/or school?

. . . .

. . . .

9. What type of training and follow-up will be provided for the entire student body in relation to the needs and safety of TGNB and/or gender questioning students in your classroom and/or school?

. . . .

. . . .

10. What are the by-laws in your school's jurisdiction that must be honored and accepted in relation to the needs and safety of TGNB and/or gender questioning students in your classroom and/or school?

. . . .

. . . .

11. How and by whom will the by-laws in your school's jurisdiction be introduced, implemented, and continuously updated for all school personnel, parents, and students in relation to the needs and safety of TGNB and/or gender questioning students in your school and/or classroom?

. . . .

. . . .

12. How will your school incorporate and support counseling, in and out of school, for TGNB and/or gender questioning students and their families, as well as resources and information for those who request these services and assistance?

. . . .

. . . .

Chapter 5

BEHAVIORS, BULLYING, SPORTS, AND BATHROOMS: IT TAKES A VILLAGE

VITAL VIGNETTE

Safety in school is something every family member expects for their child. The fulfillment of this promise to families must be presumed. As school policy makers are in command of creating guidelines that protect the well-being of all students while they attend school, it is important for them to keep in mind that TGNB students and/or those questioning their gender deserve the same assurances as their peers regarding safety. This consideration must also be extended to TGNB and/or gender questioning school personnel.

Moreover, there needs to be a complete understanding that trans girls are girls and that trans boys are boys as opposed to something opposite; therefore, honoring their affirmed gender under all circumstances is paramount. In addition, it is essential to comprehend that non-binary individuals are non-binary. Furthermore, when uncertain which choices are best for non-binary and/or gender questioning students in settings that affect their daily school lives and welfare, the student and/or their family have to be consulted and their wishes must be recognized. Without carefully implementing policies that safeguard the emotional security of TGNB students and/or those questioning their gender, productive learning may not successfully occur in a school environment.

Having the freedom to safely use bathroom facilities with dignity and lack of fear is not an outlandish or inappropriate expectation for TGNB students. There is absolutely no excuse for not allowing TGNB and/or gender questioning students to use the bathroom that aligns with their affirmed gender. Schools should no longer require TGNB students to routinely use the bathroom in the nurse's office, the faculty room, or another designated room by justifying that this practice is considered best for TGNB students' own protection and for the safety of others. In some schools, monitors are assigned to supervise inside or outside the boys or girls' bathroom to ensure the safety of TGNB students or those who, guided by misinformation and/or misconceptions, feel TGNB students will harm someone in the bathroom merely because they are trans-identified. Many schools have reached the conclusion that it is beneficial for all concerned to designate a separate gender-neutral bathroom for all TGNB students and feel this is sufficient. However, most binary bathrooms already have individual stalls that offer student privacy within the bathroom setting. Nevertheless, TGNB students often have to sprint from one end of a building to the other to use the only facility available to them.

Some parents have shared that the bathroom was so far away their child soiled themselves as they rushed as quickly as they could to reach it. Others have told stories of their child being given a late warning to class, as a result of the fact that they had to race up and down stairs or travel half-way to the other side of the school to use the designated bathroom. Furthermore, some parents have stated that their child will avoid using the bathroom altogether, in order to not be late or endure the possible stigma of using a "separate but equal" bathroom. Not only can this cause medical challenges, such as urinary tract infections, but also it may prevent a student from being able to focus on their learning. TGNB and/or gender questioning students simply want to use a bathroom for natural body functions and leave, just as non-TGNB students desire to do. If the basic act of using a bathroom that is aligned with their affirmed gender is placing them at risk, educating those who would harm them is the solution, not "separate but equal" bathrooms.

It should also be noted there are numerous schools that do not even acknowledge a TGNB student's affirmed gender and emphatically demand that a student uses the bathroom facility that solely aligns with their gender assigned at birth. Clearly, the use of a bathroom for a TGNB and/or gender questioning student is something that must be a priority. Likewise, it is key that the arrangements both follow the law and recognize this issue through the lens of a TGNB and/or gender questioning student's point of view.

This is also true in reference to locker rooms. Those who create policies for TGNB students and/or those questioning their gender need to consider that many students, on some level, may be apprehensive in the locker room. Therefore, providing multiple, individual, changing rooms and stalls for dressing and showering is ideal for personal privacy. In fact, for certain age groups of varying puberty levels, these strongly suggested guidelines can be equally relevant and appropriate for the betterment of all students as a whole, not only for those students who identify on the transgender spectrum.

It is necessary for advisors of clubs and of sports teams to pre-plan and research trans-related policies before traveling to other facilities. Making pre-arrangements that honor the safety needs of their TGNB and/or gender questioning players, as they would for any other student, is highly recommended. This policy will need to apply to day field trips and overnight activities.

Once it is known that a student is transitioning and/or questioning their gender, discussions will need to occur, acknowledging that laws will play a major role in how membership and participation on a particular sports team may be affected. Policies formed by their school will also impact this reality. The possible outcomes of them not being allowed to join or forcing their removal from a team can be devastating to the student. Some TGNB students and their families have communicated they learned to accept that until society faces the truth that TGNB and/or gender questioning students are entitled to the same rights as other students, they are willing to bear temporary accommodations for these activities only as long as safety is ensured and engagement is not prevented.

It is a given that bullying and harassment of any student, in all of their forms, are unacceptable by any individual in a school environment. One of the extra layers of difficulty that challenges TGNB students and their families is when those in charge of their safety and well-being disregard or inappropriately address a problem, sometimes under the pretext that the action was a mistake or part of the offender's learning curve. As discussed in a previous chapter, making an unintentional pronoun or name error can happen as school personnel begin incorporating these changes. Admitting this, correcting it at the time it occurs, and then moving on are all suitable ways to handle an inadvertent misstatement. However, continuously or purposely misusing these known changes should not be tolerated by any TGNB and/or gender questioning student, their family members, school employees, or volunteers. If school personnel or a student observes others laughing, verbally insulting, or clearly mocking a TGNB and/or gender questioning student, or anyone else for that matter, they have an ethical obligation to address what they have seen or heard and not be a bystander. If a TGNB student or their family member feels they have been bullied or harassed while attending school, school personnel should be able to refer to previously established protocol that is known to all. In addition, there needs to be a point person in charge, who is astutely aware of the laws and school policies that affect the rights of TGNB and/or gender questioning students. This individual, or perhaps team, must be required to understand exact and effective avenues in which to proceed with a complaint or an inquiry, never disregarding the seriousness of the situation, and be properly trained in order to address the circumstances appropriately.

Policies pertaining to issues that concern TGNB and/or gender questioning students such as, but not limited to, protection and safety, bathroom and locker room usage, the incorporation of affirmed name and pronoun, timely and accurate training of staff, students, and parents, and participation in school-related activities and clubs, need to be created. Additional policies and procedures concerning bullying and harassment that include consequences for the violation of these guidelines must be established. Furthermore, policy makers will need to continue re-evaluating, updating, and assessing these policies which must be documented and implemented within a predetermined time frame that is upheld and appropriate. It is crucial and prudent that as schools are developing these policies affecting the lives of TGNB and/or gender questioning students and their families, that they are part of the team or are respectfully consulted and heard as these mandates are finalized, prior to being implemented.

Accountable and specific procedures should be formally written and reinforced to the strictest of guidelines. Training and awareness of all school policies have to be taught, used, and enforced by all those who are employed, hired to provide services, and who volunteer in schools. The list of those who must be required to follow the laws set by governing law makers and by those who write school policies that protect the rights of TGNB and/or gender questioning students is long but vital. Ideally, the trainees will include: teachers and support staff, administrators and superintendents, custodians, nurses, school psychologists, social workers, special area teachers, physiotherapists and occupational therapists, speech and language pathologists, aides, secretaries, security, substitutes, volunteers, after-school staff, school boards, athletic coaches, drama and club leaders, scout leaders, bus drivers, cafeteria workers, recess staff, hallway and bathroom monitors, greeters, parent-teacher association members, crossing guards, all students, parents of all students, and community members who work alongside the school population. Additionally, those who may directly interact with any TGNB and/or gender questioning students, as they bring programs to the school during school hours for special events or student services such as, but not limited to, Photo and Graduation Day staff, school assemblies, Child Protective Services (if and when applicable), and outside medical or mental health professionals, will also have to follow these regulations.

In a perfect world, all these individuals would be part of the team that supports and accepts the appropriate inclusion of TGNB and/or gender questioning students. Is this realistic? Can most or at least many of these people be trained? Where does a school start? How will a school continue to update these policies? These and an abundance of other questions will need to be answered by every school. The ultimate and accurate responses to these reflective questions can only be obtained if all those who interact with students who identify as TGNB and/or questioning their gender are afforded the opportunity to learn, through proper training, the best and most respectful ways to communicate with and ensure the well-being of these students.

ANECDOTAL AFFIRMATION

ANECDOTAL AFFIRMATION

School is a place
To learn,
Teach everyone
To embrace differences,
Support and celebrate
All gender identities.

This Anecdotal Affirmation is meant to inspire, provoke thought, and empower your learning in any way that opens your heart. Its presence is intended to set the tone and intention of the chapter. This affirmation may be used as a springboard for writing or as a conversation starter with someone else. Ample space has been provided for you to reflect on the Anecdotal Affirmation.

GRAPHICS GALORE

Splash

Can you jot down all of the words and terms that would be considered hurtful to TGNB and/or gender questioning students? As you brainstorm, write your words and terms quickly by randomly scattering them anywhere on the page in a splash-like manner. Use the information obtained from the *Splash* to assess what words and terms you already know are hurtful in relation to these students.

REFLECTIVE RESPONSES

1. What are your school policies and procedures in relation to bathroom and locker room use for TGNB and/or gender questioning students?

....

....

....

....

....

....

....

....

2. How and who will train all school personnel about school policies and procedures in relation to bathroom and locker room use for TGNB and/or gender questioning students?

....

....

....

....

....

....

....

3. What are your school policies and procedures in relation to TGNB and/ or gender questioning students when playing sports?

....

....

....

....

....

....

....

....

4. How and who will train all school personnel about school policies and procedures in relation to TGNB and/or gender questioning students when playing sports?

....

....

....

....

....

....

....

....

5. How will challenges and conflicts about school policies and procedures be resolved in relation to issues pertinent to TGNB and/or gender questioning students?

. . . .

. . . .

. . . .

. . . .

. . . .

. . . .

. . . .

. . . .

6. What are your school's policies and procedures regarding bullying and harassment behaviors in relation to TGNB and/or gender questioning students?

. . . .

. . . .

. . . .

. . . .

. . . .

. . . .

. . . .

7. How and who will train all students about school policies and procedures regarding bullying and harassment in relation to TGNB and/or gender questioning students?

. . . .

. . . .

. . . .

. . . .

. . . .

. . . .

. . . .

8. How will challenges and conflicts about school policies and procedures regarding bullying and harassment in relation to TGNB and/or gender questioning students be addressed after training occurs and how will the person or team in charge of assisting in these matters become known to all school personnel?

. . . .

. . . .

. . . .

. . . .

. . . .

. . . .

. . . .

9. How and who will offer training to all parents about school policies and procedures regarding bathroom and locker room use, issues concerning team sports, as well as bullying and harassment in relation to TGNB and/or gender questioning students?

. . . .

. . . .

. . . .

. . . .

. . . .

. . . .

. . . .

10. How will parents, guardians, caregivers, students, and family members of TGNB and/ or gender questioning students be included and part of the conversation when training, policies, procedures, and guidelines are created, implemented, and updated?

. . . .

. . . .

. . . .

. . . .

. . . .

. . . .

. . . .

11. How can local community members and outside organizations be provided with an opportunity to serve and play a role in supporting the safety and rights of the school's TGNB and/or gender questioning students?

....

....

....

....

....

....

....

....

12. How can those in the Trans community be provided with an opportunity to serve and play a role in supporting the safety and rights of the school's TGNB and/or gender questioning students?

....

....

....

....

....

....

....

GAME

Matching Pre-Test 4

It is important to be aware of what you know and to use that knowledge as a starting point to grow. After taking the pre-test, you will realize what you still need to learn. The tools in this chapter were created to help you internalize the vocabulary. As a pre-test, match the vocabulary (the numbers) with the definitions (the letters) by drawing a line from a number to a letter. Each number and letter should only be used once. What were your results? The answer keys are provided in the Answer Key section in Chapter 8. It is suggested that you check your answers after you have taken the pre-test to see how well you did. Feel free to repeat this process at a later time; you may choose to use this activity to assess your progress by using this game as a post-test.

1. LGBTQQIA+ (also LGBTQ and LGBTQ+)	A. A person who is in a sexual and/or romantic relationship with someone.
2. metoidioplasty	B. An abbreviation that describes a person who now identifies as female gendered but was assigned a male gender at birth.
3. misogyny	C. The use of prosthetics and other materials to enable an individual to possess the appearance and feeling of having a penis and testicles.
4. monogamous	D. A disdain, hatred, or mistrust of all people female and feminine.
5. MTF/M2F/FTF/male-to-female	E. A type of bottom surgery that involves the removal of testicles.
6. non-binary	F. The act of disclosing someone's sexuality and/or gender identity without their knowledge and/or permission.
7. orchiectomy	G. A gender that is not exclusively male or exclusively female and is outside the gender binary.
8. outing	H. A gender-affirming bottom surgery which releases the micro phallus and can include urethra lengthening.
9. packing	I. A type of relationship where a person is sexually and/or romantically involved with only one person at a time.
10. pan hysterectomy	J. A type of bottom surgery that usually includes removing the uterus, ovaries, and fallopian tubes and which could involve the removal of the cervix.
11. pansexual	K. An all-encompassing abbreviation which stands for lesbian, gay, bisexual, transgender, queer, questioning, intersex, allies, plus others.
12. partner	L. Someone who is attracted to people of various genders.

Retake this pre-test as a post-test to assess your personal progress and knowledge.

EMPATHY-EMBRACING EXERCISE

For many transgender, non-binary, and/or gender questioning people, the fear of losing the respect and support of family and friends can prevent them from disclosing their affirmed gender. This also holds true for students disclosing their affirmed gender at school.

Was there ever a time in your life that you feared losing the respect and support of those in school if you disclosed something personal about yourself? If so, what was it and did you disclose it? If not, why? If yes, what was the outcome?

GRAPHICS GALORE

Timeline

When an incident occurs involving any student, it is usually recommended that a guidance counselor and/or mental health professional working for the school district be notified. This is especially true for situations that involve any type of bullying or harassment that affects TGNB and/or gender questioning students, for there are often laws and rights that must not be violated or ignored. To assist in the recording process, this *Timeline* graphic organizer has been created to help guidance counselors and mental health professionals understand what is necessary to include when documenting any type of incident. This format would also be ideal to be used by all school personnel when logging any inappropriate action taken against any student in the school setting, in case the specific details are needed in the future. It is suggested that you make copies of this graphic prior to its use, in order for you to have the original available at another time. You may opt to use a separate form for each individual involved. Whenever possible, state a detailed description of each individual next to their name, if applicable to the question.

Who was involved?
Date:

What happened?
Date:

Where did it happen?
Date:

Why did it happen?
Date:

Were the proper people notified of the situation, and if so, who were they?
Date:

How was it/will it be resolved?
Date:

DESERVING DE-STRESSING DELIGHT

Date with Yourself

Make a date with yourself, which can lovingly be called "Getting to Know Yourself." Making a date with yourself can be quite a liberating and exhilarating experience but can also feel strange and scary. Taking time to reflect on all the decisions that require your energy, as educators, can be exhausting. If you are the type of person who craves the company of others, it might surprise you if you ever find that you have the yearning to spend periods of time by yourself. Perhaps this will possibly be due to your desire to explore your individual journey as you expand your mind and educational philosophies about things you had never thought about in the past. Make a list of the things you enjoy and then attempt doing one or two of them. You may like to write in solitude or prefer to reflect as you experience an activity on your own, such as a sporting event, a museum tour, or a music concert.

Some people elect to take a mini-vacation alone, while others tell those in their lives that they are away on vacation, but in actuality stay at home and do not respond to outside communication. Those with financial obstacles can search for free events happening in their area. One person shared with me that they went alone for a quiet bike ride by a lake for several hours and then stopped to paint with water colors to capture what they had seen. All of these self-dates are offered only as examples of how beautiful the experience can be to explore your own thoughts through "Getting to Know Yourself" dates. Find what you love to do and then discover those hidden spaces and bravely unwrap them. As you date yourself from time to time, you can find exactly what you seek, for all the answers are inside you right now!

Journal your reaction to this Deserving De-Stressing Delight.

GAME

Three-in-a-Row

All players write nine of the vocabulary words from the *Mix-n-Match* game directly onto the empty spaces of a blank *Three-in-a-Row* board. One player reads the vocabulary definition cards aloud. If a player's *Three-in-a-Row* board has the vocabulary word that matches the vocabulary definition that was just read, the player puts a coin or placeholder onto the corresponding vocabulary word on their *Three-in-a-Row* board. Once a player's *Three-in-a-Row* board contains three placeholders in a row, they are the winner and verbally state: *Three-in-a-Row!* The player who reads the vocabulary definitions may opt to have their own *Three-in-a-Row* board, too. Should all or some of the players prefer to each take a turn reading the vocabulary definitions aloud, this option may also work well. An alternative is to have a player verbally state the vocabulary word and then players mark the matching vocabulary word on their *Three-in-a-Row* board. Another version is to have a player read the vocabulary words and the players mark the corresponding vocabulary definitions on their *Three-in-a-Row* board. It should be noted that each player will need to have written the vocabulary definitions onto the nine empty spaces of a blank *Three-in-a-Row* board prior to playing this version of the game.

Supplies: Each player begins with a *Three-in-a-Row* board and nine coins or other placeholders. You may copy the *Three-in-a-Row* board from the workbook for the sole purpose of playing this game.

Suggestion: Feel free to make six to ten copies of the *Three-in-a-Row* board below!

GRAPHICS GALORE

T-Chart

Write down what specific policies and procedures you **"Know"** your school currently has in place in relation to addressing the needs of TGNB and/or gender questioning students, what you **"Want"** to be in place, and what you have **"Learned"** needs to be in place for the safety and welfare of these students.

Topic	Know	Want	Learned
1.			
2.			
3.			
4.			
5.			
6.			
7.			

SAMPLER SHARE

I am submitting my own reply to the Reflective Responses question listed below as a sample, hoping to inspire you to use it as a springboard to formulate your own practices. Please be aware that all of the students' names have been removed, as well as most of the actual pronouns for the student and parent, in order to respect the privacy of TGNB and/or gender questioning students, their parents, and other family members. It should be noted that all of these methods can be beneficial for all students, not only those who identify as TGNB and/or are questioning their gender. It is imperative to understand that even without intending to, gender-based practices can negatively impact the social and emotional well-being of students who identify on the transgender spectrum. For these reasons and the need to be transparent, samples are incorporated that portray how the lives of gender-diverse students were also affected, though they did not identify themselves as TGNB and/or gender questioning at the time of the event. Whether they do now, or not, is unknown.

How can local community members and outside organizations be provided with an opportunity to serve and play a role in supporting the safety and rights of the school's TGNB and/or gender questioning students?

Most schools hire outside groups to present assembly programs to the entire school population and this was the case for the school in which I was employed when I had a young, shy student who was AFAB (Assigned Female At Birth); however, their gender expression was more aligned with masculine aspects of gender. There were days of anticipation leading up to the big event, for the outside organization had sent a packet to all the classroom teachers encouraging them to prepare the students for the presentation. This particular student was probably the most excited, for the topic was of great interest to them. We all walked happily down to the gymnasium where the performance was going to occur and this student elected to sit front and center in order to not miss a word of it. Halfway through the program, the lead performer stated he needed six assistants from the audience to help him with an activity. He expressed that he needed volunteers who could pay attention, follow directions, and were sitting properly in the audience.

Much to my surprise and joy, this timid student raised their hand, hoping beyond hope to be chosen. One by one the lead performer chose the first five children and requested that the pool of students lower their voices, for many were shouting with an enthusiastic plea to be selected. As he walked around the room in search for the last participant, he announced that he already had two boys and three girls, so he was looking for another boy. As the performer quickly noticed the respectful manner in which my AFAB student was behaving and following the directive to be seated quietly, the performer broadcasted to the entire student body he was going to select that particular student, whom the performer clearly thought was a boy. The AFAB student was humiliated as their peers began to laugh aloud and chant, "She's not a boy, she's a girl!" This spirited, innocent student buried their head in shame and understandably so, refused to go on stage. My heart sank, as did many other educators in the audience.

When we returned to the class, we all talked about what had happened and many peers supported this student by sharing stories of when they felt embarrassed or made fun of at school. Not only did I speak with the presenter who apologetically spoke to the student with me there, but he vowed never to select a student from the audience again based on gender. From that day forward, whenever an outside organization came to perform for the school, I made it my business to speak to as many groups as possible about never choosing a student from the audience by using gender as a criterion or assuming anyone's gender, including the gender of school personnel.

GRAPHICS GALORE

Bar Graph

Based on a scale from 1 to 10, with 1 being the lowest and 10 being the highest, color or shade in your response. This visual will illustrate where your greatest concerns lie and can be used as a tool to help you communicate your thoughts with trainers, colleagues, administrators, parents, and students (if and when appropriate), or for your own personal understanding. The bar graph results can vary as you learn more about the Trans community, or your thinking shifts. It is critical that educators process and reflect on their feelings about the specifics of the policies that will affect the lives of students who identify as TGNB and/or gender questioning. More importantly, educators must overcome their own possible conflicting beliefs to ensure that they always treat all students with the dignity and respect they deserve.

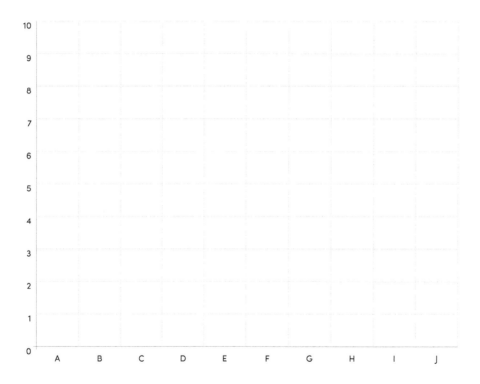

To what degree are these policy issues important to you in relation to TGNB and/or gender questioning student's safety in school? The polices your school has in relation to...

A. Bullying of TGNB students.

B. Harassment of TGNB students.

C. Inclusive bathroom use for TGNB students.

D. Inclusive locker room use for TGNB students.

E. Inclusive sports for TGNB students.

F. Inclusive clubs and/or activities for TGNB students.

G. Addressing inclusiveness for TGNB students at proms or gendered parties.

H. Inclusive overnight accommodations for TGNB students.

I. Inclusive dressing room use in regard to theater productions for TGNB students.

J. Addressing inclusive bathroom use prior to classes participating in field trips and/or off-site swimming lessons for TGNB students.

ANECDOTAL AFFIRMATION

ANECDOTAL AFFIRMATION

Each challenge
Is met with bravery,
Each obstacle
Is met with courage,
Each battle
Is met with
Inner strength.

This Anecdotal Affirmation is meant to inspire, provoke thought, and empower your learning in any way that opens your heart. Its presence is intended to set the tone and intention of the chapter. This affirmation may be used as a springboard for writing or as a conversation starter with someone else. Ample space has been provided for you to reflect on the Anecdotal Affirmation.

COMMUNICATION CORNER

Reflecting on your own thoughts and experiences is critical when processing new information and adjusting your thinking. Equally important can be sharing and learning how others analyze their own thoughts and experiences. This exercise was designed with the intention of offering teachers, support staff, and administrators a safe place to discuss all the topics addressed in this chapter. When two or more school employees candidly begin a conversation that embraces an open dialogue without judgment or criticism of one another's beliefs and ideas concerning students and school policies, everyone benefits. It is suggested that after teachers, support staff, and administrators privately answer the questions from the Reflective Responses section, they converse about one or two of them, while others may prefer to answer them all with a trusted colleague or administrator. In order to recall the questions you answered, simply highlight or circle the ones you addressed and then ask others the ones they responded to on their own. By doing so in a respectful and communicative manner that honors the voices of all those working or interacting with the students who identify as transgender, non-binary, and/or are questioning their gender, teachers, support staff, and administrators in your school can positively impact the lives of the students they are committed to serve as professionals. Do you and your colleague or administrator answer these questions in the same way or differently? Discuss your responses to understand how all of you view the answers to the questions and make time to celebrate all you learn from being willing to communicate with one another.

1. What are your school policies and procedures in relation to bathroom and locker room use for TGNB and/or gender questioning students?

   . . . .

   . . . .

2. How and who will train all school personnel about school policies and procedures in relation to bathroom and locker room use for TGNB and/or gender questioning students?

   . . . .

   . . . .

3. What are your school policies and procedures in relation to TGNB and/ or gender questioning students when playing sports?

....

....

4. How and who will train all school personnel about school policies and procedures in relation to TGNB and/or gender questioning students when playing sports?

....

....

5. How will challenges and conflicts about school policies and procedures be resolved in relation to issues pertinent to TGNB and/or gender questioning students?

....

....

6. What are your school's policies and procedures regarding bullying and harassment behaviors in relation to TGNB and/or gender questioning students?

....

....

7. How and who will train all students about school policies and procedures regarding bullying and harassment in relation to TGNB and/or gender questioning students?

....

....

8. How will challenges and conflicts about school policies and procedures regarding bullying and harassment in relation to TGNB and/or gender questioning students be addressed after training occurs and how will the person or team in charge of assisting in these matters become known to all school personnel?

. . . .

. . . .

9. How and who will offer training to all parents about school policies and procedures regarding bathroom and locker room use, issues concerning team sports, as well as bullying and harassment in relation to TGNB and/or gender questioning students?

. . . .

. . . .

10. How will parents, guardians, caregivers, students, and family members of TGNB and/or gender questioning students be included and part of the conversation when training, policies, procedures, and guidelines are created, implemented, and updated?

. . . .

. . . .

11. How can local community members and outside organizations be provided with an opportunity to serve and play a role in supporting the safety and rights of the school's TGNB and/or gender questioning students?

. . . .

. . . .

12. How can those in the Trans community be provided with an opportunity to serve and play a role in supporting the safety and rights of the school's TGNB and/or gender questioning students?

. . . .

. . . .

Chapter 6

VIEWING PRACTICES AND CURRICULUM WHILE CREATING A CULTURE OF INCLUSION

VITAL VIGNETTE

Until now, most of the information or policies discussed thus far could be pertinent to all school personnel. This chapter is different. Its primary focus is on teachers and support staff, though certain recommendations may require consultation with administrators before implementation. There are concrete and appropriate ways classroom teachers and support staff may adjust their teaching to embrace practices that will not only enhance the learning and well-being of TGNB students and/or those questioning their gender, but also all learners within the classroom setting, while promoting gender equity to achieve gender equality. Some of the suggestions will apply to all those who work in any classroom regardless of the grade level. Other ideas can be more relevant to one age group instead of another; however, with a little creativity, most proposals may be modified and used by all those who wish to benefit from them. Though many of these submissions can become part of the guidelines a school adopts, teachers may elect to implement them in their own classroom before, or if, they become mandated policies.

Learning more about your students' needs in relation to themselves early on in the school year, or prior to them entering your classroom, can assist you as an educator to create a compassionate atmosphere for all those under your care. For this reason, whenever possible, it is advised that teachers send a questionnaire home to parents and guardians asking them the name and pronoun their child uses and should be called by and referred to by all peers and school personnel. It is understood that mailing these questionnaires home prior to the start of school may not be viable due to a number of factors. Teachers can opt to ask parents to fill out the questionnaire on Meet-the-Teacher Night, which usually happens within the first few weeks of school. If parents and guardians cannot attend this event, students can bring the questionnaire home. It is prudent to have the questionnaires translated into all languages spoken in students' homes so parents, guardians, caregivers, and students can read the questions in their native language. For those students who are old enough to respond to the questionnaire in a written form, teachers may elect to have all students fill it out themselves during the first week of school.

Though the information they share may not be legally stated on their official documentation, parents and students' wishes should be honored and verbally used. Additionally, and most respectfully, their affirmed name and pronoun should be listed on all seating charts, classroom assignments, substitute plans, name tags, permission slips, and materials hung in the classroom and the school, as well as given to all after-school programs and school personnel who interact with them for any reason. If at all feasible and aligned with school policies, these two pieces of information should be changed or added on all school computer logins and acknowledged on all personal files including Individualized Educational Plans (IEP) and medical records. It is understood that, for legal purposes, some of these recommendations may not be granted. However, when humanly possible, all efforts need to be made to do so in order to preserve the dignity and safety of a student.

In fact, it is also helpful to include questions to learn more about your students' interests, what they do in their free time, and their family dynamics. These personal insights can be useful to an educator when planning activities, center work, and class groupings. In terms of intersectionality, it is imperative for teachers and support staff to approach a person or an issue through the lens that considers the multi-dimensional, wide-ranging identities, and social-political times in which they live. Some educators may make assumptions based on a student's race, religion, height, body size/type, heritage/culture, gender, sexual orientation, class/socio-economic status, level of education, career, ability, marital status/arrangement, number of children, political affiliation, and immigration status that can be inaccurate and not aligned with how they deserve to be seen. By comprehending the role this plays in a school's culture, teachers will be able to better address the needs of all students in their classroom and educate the whole child.

When teachers create seating arrangements, they often have a specific objective or two for placing students where they do. Sometimes one of these reasons is based on gender, and so it is critical to know how a child identifies prior to assigning these placements. As a rule, be aware that for certain students this identification can be fluid and/or questioning; therefore it is strongly suggested that a variety of configurations be considered. If students are seated in groups around tables, there should be a mixture of genders at each table. If behavior is a concern, then you may elect to designate a specific seat for a student. Since grouping is often based on precise data and for a known set of criteria that is guided by a student's needs, it is recommended that educators be aware of the gender identity composition of their groupings and consider balancing the cluster of students. It is understood that this may not always be realistic, but keeping gender identity as one piece of information when forming groups can be more important to students than teachers may realize.

If classroom jobs are part of the daily routine within the classroom, it is advisable to allow a student to select the job that appeals to them, not expect them to select a job simply based on gender. Another method is to place all the students' names in a bag and randomly pick one name at a time and match it to a classroom task. Some teachers allow students to trade jobs on their own. It is optimal to grant each student the option of declining one match up in case they feel uncomfortable with this assignment.

Many teachers seem to line students up according to the gender binary and this can cause much angst to students who identify as non-binary and/or are questioning their gender. If the goal is to simply move from one location to the other, educators are urged to ask students to form one line to avoid the binary challenge for students. In addition, if having the students create two lines on their own, teachers can use this opportunity to reinforce the mathematical concepts of one-to-one correspondence, longer vs. shorter, more than, less than, equal to, and possibly multiplication tables of two, for the configuration will vary. As a result, this strategy can have a positive impact on academic learning, as well as preserving the dignity of all students.

Feeling or being excluded can have a negative impact on a student's self-esteem and self-worth. Moreover, only offering options based on preconceived binary stereotypes may foster frustration, confusion, and resentment for all those on whom they are thrust. For these reasons and several more, it is recommended that some traditional philosophies and practices be amended and updated. It is customary for parents of students in grades PreK–5 to ask that teachers physically or digitally forward birthday party invitations to specific students in their classroom, therefore excluding others. Quite often, the list of students provided to the teacher is aligned with the gender of the student who is hosting the party and not necessarily based on those friends that the birthday celebrant is close to socially. As a result, and having recognized this, some teachers require that in order for them to become involved, invitations must be sent to all students. If this plea becomes a financial burden to a parent, teachers may inquire how many students the host can afford to include and then ask the parent to converse with their child to find out those students they truly consider their friends. To the amazement of many parents, students usually state that they are friends with peers of varying gender identities. For students who identify as TGNB and/or gender questioning, this simple change enables these students to be included as well and to embrace the joy of their friendships without being overlooked because they may not identify along the binary. This strategy should also be considered when parents request that teachers send them names of classmates for the purposes of setting up playdates for their child. These classroom practices can easily be explained at Meet-the-Teacher Night and parent conferences.

Along the same lines, sometimes parents send in holiday gifts and cards, labeled "boy" or "girl" items. Instead of this common tradition, it is advised that parents send in unlabeled gifts and cards that are simply signed from their child. Once these items are brought to school, the teacher can place all the gifts and cards in a pile and students can be asked to select the gift and card of their choice. In addition, should any school personnel elect to offer students an earned reward or birthday celebratory item, this procedure would also apply. Some parents and even educators would be surprised that there are students who would not choose any one of them based on the binary or stereotypical assumptions. This method promotes individuality and choice preferences, and celebrates personal differences in a respectful manner for all students in the classroom.

Offering students options based on their likes rather than their gender assigned at birth, which is often founded on stereotypes and outdated criteria, needs to be front and center to support the climate of today. Regardless of a student's age, this mindset must take hold in order to understand the best way to value the needs of all students. Steering a student toward one particular activity, station, or center work, according to their gender identity can limit a student academically, socially, and emotionally. For some educators, this will be a new way of thinking and at moments may cause an uncomfortable feeling for those who are used to a more traditional point of view. For other teachers, this will seem an obvious and an easy fit without reservation or discomfort. Irrespective of where an educator stands, the end goal is to create a classroom and school environment that sees students as they ought to be seen without exception. If a student is insulted for selecting the color of an item that differs from Western culture binary choices and that some in society feel is inappropriate, it is the responsibility of the teacher to be a role model by protecting the safety, pride, and worthiness of the student who is being teased. The individual who may use hurtful language and gestures toward a student who is being true to themselves must be taught why this type of behavior will not be tolerated within the classroom or school setting, while never embarrassing or ridiculing them for doing so.

Besides learning not to mock the color choices of peers, students will need to be educated as to the fact that all games and activities may be played and used by all students without regard to gender. Likewise, derogatory and offensive words and terms, even if they are used at home and in the media, cannot be deemed as acceptable under any circumstances, including in a joking manner. Expressions such as "That's so gay!" and "Decide if you are a boy or girl!" must have no place in school. It may seem insignificant but statements such as those can be very damaging and hurtful not only to the student being ridiculed but also to all students in the school. Intentional or not, these remarks should never be admissible in any school environment, whether the words are initiated by an adult or a student. Teachers, support staff, and administrators alike must lead the way in voicing their objections without any hesitation.

Special area teachers play a key role in a student's education and this can never be minimized. They must always be included in discussions that involve personal information about students. Equally important is how these educators use this vital knowledge when teaching the student body. Library media specialists should incorporate these strategies as well. Since these specialists are often the ones who order the books that the majority of students borrow and are the most knowledgeable on the wide variety of literature in the market, it is essential that they purchase resources that appropriately portray TGNB and/or gender questioning individuals. These materials need to be readily available and visibly displayed so that all students have access to them. By doing so, library media specialists will be acknowledging the presence of trans-identified and/or gender questioning students in school in an accepting manner.

Art teachers can contribute in supporting TGNB and/or gender questioning students by exposing students to artists who identify outside the gender binary. Moreover, they are encouraged to display paintings, sculptures, and photographs that exhibit different genders as well as various shaped and sized bodies to enable all students to be aware of, embrace, and celebrate the various genders and forms of the human body. Music teachers, especially prior to voices changing, should consider not designating girl and boy vocal parts. Whenever possible, theater teachers can introduce the concept of reversing and expanding traditional roles usually assigned to a specific gender. Physical education teachers need to be acutely aware of locker room challenges for TGNB and/or gender questioning students and help create school policies that are inclusive for all students. This also applies to the requirement of changing into bathing suits for swimming classes on and off school grounds. Furthermore, drama teachers must investigate the policies in regard to dressing areas for theatrical performances and follow the same protocol established for all students in the production. On field days and for other events or activities, forming teams solely or primarily along the gender binary can be debilitating for TGNB students and/or those who are questioning their gender, possibly discouraging and even preventing them from participating.

For any student, having representation of themselves in school settings is critical in building self-confidence, boosting self-worth, and validating gender identity. Most books classroom teachers assign or read aloud to students reinforce the notion that a person is either male or female. Rarely, if ever, are there books assigned or read to students in school that portray images of any characters who identify as TGNB and/or are questioning their gender. With a few exceptions, especially those geared toward young people, literature is limited in its depiction of TGNB and/or gender questioning individuals. In order to counter this imbalance and recognize those students who align themselves along the gender continuum, teachers have an obligation to question and whenever possible, encourage students to think outside the gender binary and oppose gender stereotypes on any level. To do so, when reading books aloud, teachers can temporarily change the name of a character to a gender-neutral name, use the pronouns of "they/them/their," and allow students to decide for themselves the gender of a character. Once students express the gender of a character, educators can ask, "Why do you think that character is a boy? Would you explain your reasons for believing that character is a girl? What makes you say that you cannot tell the character's gender from what we have just read? Does anyone else feel differently about that character's gender and can you tell us why?" Once challenged and confronted with the way stereotypes of gender are portrayed in literature, in addition to how past learning has impacted their beliefs, all students can begin to embrace the fact that everyone should have the opportunity to see themselves in books, educational materials, and the media. Fortunately, there are some children's books and resources that incorporate TGNB and/or gender questioning characters, as well as age-appropriate ones, which explore the topic of gender in a sensitive manner and are both informative and thought-provoking while preserving the integrity of all students. It should be acknowledged that when discussing books in regard to TGNB and/or gender questioning characters takes place, those students who identify on the transgender spectrum must never be referred to, talked about, or singled out in any manner that would be different from those who do not identify in this way.

Educators need to integrate simple yet powerful practices that respect the diversity of gender identifications in all subject areas. Accurate LGBTQQIA+ history must also be included within the curriculum that history teachers use in their classroom and this must not be in the form of an honorable mention. There have been key LGBTQQIA+ figures who have made major contributions to society in terms of activism and politics, professional fields, the arts, military services, and a myriad of other essential areas. By validating the important role LGBTQQIA+ individuals have performed in the world throughout history and not forgetting to incorporate the significant part those in the Trans community have played, educators are exposing all students to a more complete record of the past and ensuring that LGBTQQIA+ history is no longer absent from the school curriculum. When sex education is taught in schools, the lesson/s should not only be focused on that of cisgender, straight students. School health educators must also include the sexual wellness of LGBTQQIA+ needs and perspectives, including material about pregnancy relating to TGNB and/or intersex students. It must be noted that students who are intersex may or may not identify on the transgender spectrum. Biology classes would be wise to include hormone and genital information that impact the bodies of TGNB and/or gender questioning students, as well as those who are intersex.

Just as a TGNB student's name and pronoun need to be aligned with their affirmed gender in all settings, foreign language classes must do the same when precise gender-based words are involved. Though some foreign languages do not have gender-specific language rules, others do. If a student identifies as TGNB and/or is questioning their gender, foreign language teachers have to address and refer to the student with their gender-affirming name and pronoun both in and out of the classroom. This action must occur at all times, with the acute awareness that not doing so could cause these students much emotional distress and social embarrassment. As in all other situations and for all students, if a teacher is unsure of the name and pronoun a student uses, they should ask the student this information privately in order to preserve everyone's dignity.

Instead of only using "she/her/hers" and "he/him/his" pronouns in word problems, "they/them/their" pronouns should also be used in examples such as: "Chris had three toy cars and two small dolls; how many did they have in all?" Plus, teachers may choose to eliminate the "boy" or "girl" type of labeling when it is not critical to an objective. Some elementary school teachers have been known to begin the year graphing the number of boys in the class versus the number of girls in the class. If the objective is to teach the concept of graphing, there are many more topics and ways to do this. Is it truly vital information for the students in the classroom to know the status of each other's gender? How is this information relevant to students? Should educators and/or students feel this is important data to post in some capacity around the room, whether in a graphing format or not, there needs to be a respectful discussion about those who do not identify on the binary. Furthermore, when students are addressed as a whole, wording such as "boys and girls" or "ladies and gentlemen" can be replaced or alternated with words like "friends," "everyone," "people," "everybody," and even "folks," for all of these choices are implicitly gender neutral.

In regard to posting on any form of social media, no student should be outed or placed in a position to be exposed in any manner that does not respect their affirmed gender, whether orally or visually. This holds true for photos and videos displayed in the classroom and throughout the school. As a student transitions, images that reflect their affirmed gender will need to be updated before they are presented in public and only after permission is granted for them to be used, for there can be no exception to this protocol. There are many teachers who create videos, slide shows, and photo exhibits for holidays and end-of-year celebrations without realizing that a TGNB and/or gender questioning student's voice or image portrayed in these projects may not be appropriately aligned with their affirmed gender. It is highly recommended that a student who is in transition is privately consulted as to which images and type of media they are comfortable having displayed for events, for their wishes need to be completely respected.

In summary, an inclusive curriculum must be put in place for those students who are in transition, identify as TGNB, and/or are questioning their gender. If this does not occur, these students may become emotionally harmed. Any indication that the underlying message of being true to themselves is not acceptable can leave them vulnerable to peer ridicule and isolation. The examples and recommendations stated above are intended to be viewed as a starting point, especially for those educators who are seeking guidance. Incorporating one or two suggestions, weekly or monthly, is a laudable beginning and will make a difference in the school's culture. Reflecting on, revising, and enhancing these ideas will all be part of the educational process. Little by little, positive changes will occur in the classroom. When educators consciously include the voices of TGNB and/or gender questioning students, everyone has the opportunity to be visible, acknowledged, and heard by all in every school setting.

ANECDOTAL AFFIRMATION

ANECDOTAL AFFIRMATION

We must
Teach others,
So one day,
Everyone
Will have learned!

This Anecdotal Affirmation is meant to inspire, provoke thought, and empower your learning in any way that opens your heart. Its presence is intended to set the tone and intention of the chapter. This affirmation may be used as a springboard for writing or as a conversation starter with someone else. Ample space has been provided for you to reflect on the Anecdotal Affirmation.

GRAPHICS GALORE

Splash

Can you jot down the books that you use, assign, and read to the students in your classroom every year? As you brainstorm, write the book titles quickly by randomly scattering them anywhere on the page in a splash-like manner. Use the information obtained from the *Splash* to assess if the books you already use, assign, and read every year support the inclusion and needs of TGNB and/or gender questioning students in relation to classroom lessons and curriculum.

REFLECTIVE RESPONSES

1. What aspects of your practices being used in your classroom specifically address the needs, inclusion, and acceptance of TGNB and/or gender questioning students?

....

....

....

....

....

....

....

....

2. What aspects of the practices being used throughout the school specifically address the needs, inclusion, and acceptance of TGNB and/or gender questioning students?

....

....

....

....

....

....

....

....

3. What aspects of the current curriculum and lesson plans being used in your classroom specifically address the needs, inclusion, and acceptance of TGNB and/or gender questioning students?

....

....

....

....

....

....

....

....

4. What aspects of the current curriculum and lesson plans being used throughout the school specifically address the needs, inclusion, and acceptance of TGNB and/or gender questioning students?

....

....

....

....

....

....

....

....

5. What aspects of the current curriculum and lesson plans being used in your classroom do you now recognize require adjustments in order to address the needs, inclusion, and acceptance of TGNB and/or gender questioning students?

....

....

....

....

....

....

....

6. What aspects of the current curriculum and lesson plans being used throughout the school do you now recognize require adjustments in order to address the needs, inclusion, and acceptance of TGNB and/or gender questioning students?

....

....

....

....

....

....

....

7. What aspects of the current literature and materials being used in your classroom do you now recognize require adjustments in order to address the needs, inclusion, and acceptance of TGNB and/or gender questioning students?

. . . .

. . . .

. . . .

. . . .

. . . .

. . . .

. . . .

8. What aspects of the current literature and materials being used throughout the school do you now recognize require adjustments in order to address the needs, inclusion, and acceptance of TGNB and/or gender questioning students?

. . . .

. . . .

. . . .

. . . .

. . . .

. . . .

. . . .

9. How has the intersectionality of your identities influenced your interactions and educational practices in the classroom with TGNB and/or gender questioning students?

....

....

....

....

....

....

....

....

10. What can you and your colleagues do to ensure the needs, inclusion, and acceptance of the TGNB and/or gender questioning students in your classroom and/or school?

....

....

....

....

....

....

....

....

11. What do you feel administrators can do to ensure the needs, inclusion, and acceptance of the TGNB and/or gender questioning students in your classroom and/or school?

....

....

....

....

....

....

....

12. What do you feel the student body can do to ensure the needs, inclusion, and acceptance of the TGNB and/or gender questioning students in your classroom and/or school?

....

....

....

....

....

....

....

GAME

Matching Pre-Test 5

It is important to be aware of what you know and to use that knowledge as a starting point to grow. After taking the pre-test, you will realize what you still need to learn. The tools in this chapter were created to help you internalize the vocabulary. As a pre-test, match the vocabulary (the numbers) with the definitions (the letters) by drawing a line from a number to a letter. Each number and letter should only be used once. What were your results? The answer keys are provided in the Answer Key section in Chapter 8. It is suggested that you check your answers after you have taken the pre-test to see how well you did. Feel free to repeat this process at a later time; you may choose to use this activity to assess your progress by using this game as a post-test.

1. passing	A. The ability for a person to be read as their affirmed gender by those who are unaware that the individual's identity is transgender.
2. phalloplasty	B. The practice of using or referring to a person in the way an individual needs to be addressed, also known as proper gender pronouns.
3. POC	C. A term for a medicine that blocks the hormone GnRH (Gonadotropin Releasing Hormone).
4. polyamorous	D. The act of a person who is attempting to figure out their own sexuality and/or gender.
5. preferred gender pronouns	E. A surgical procedure that creates a scrotal sac and can include testicular implants.
6. puberty blockers	F. A word that refers to a sexual orientation that is not heterosexual and/or anything that is non-heteronormative.
7. queer	G. An abbreviation that stands for a Person/People of Color.
8. questioning	H. A system to classify the development of puberty in children.
9. scrotoplasty	I. The pattern of thoughts, feelings, and arousal that determine sexual preferences.
10. sexuality	J. A type of relationship where a person is sexually and/or romantically involved with more than one person at the same time.
11. stealth	K. A word used for a transgender person who chooses to keep their trans status private.
12. Tanner stages	L. A type of bottom surgery that entails the construction of a penis and can include the construction of testicles and the implant of an erection device.

Retake this pre-test as a post-test to assess your personal progress and knowledge.

EMPATHY-EMBRACING EXERCISE

School can feel like a home away from home to some students, while it can be a place that is alienating and scary for others. Feeling accepted, respected, and included for being exactly who you are as a person are often factors that determine which reality becomes a student's experience. Most teachers, support staff, and administrators can relate to one of these feelings and it may trigger memories from their past. Succeeding both academically and emotionally throughout your school life is the hope and desired outcome for those students who attend school. Unfortunately, for many students who identify on the transgender spectrum and/or are questioning their gender, being asked to compromise who you are can become a daily struggle. However, sometimes being motivated to rise above such adversity and learning to function has enabled people to thrive and achieve. Knowing that there is a support team that can provide a sense of community for trans students can make all the difference and it can save a life!

Can you remember a time when you were not accepted, respected, or included in school for any reason beyond your control? How did this make you feel? Were you able to overcome these feelings of rejection? If so, how did you overcome this and did the support of others play any role in helping you be the person you are today?

GRAPHICS GALORE

Box

State the different ways to describe your intersecting identities by placing one answer in each box. The placement of your responses and the ones you elect to state do not necessarily need to be completed in any order, unless you prefer to rank your answers 1-25 with 1 being the most important way to identify yourself and 25 being the least important way to identify yourself in relation to the others. This graphic organizer can help you understand if your intersectionality affected/affects your life choices and how you and others view you. The intersection of your identities plays a role in how you relate to your TGNB and/or gender questioning students, as well as other students and co-workers. (Optional examples: race, color, religion, height, body size/type, heritage/culture, gender, sexual orientation, class/socio-economic status, level of education, career, ability, marital status/arrangement, number of children, political affiliation, immigration status, etc.)

1	2	3	4	5
6	7	8	9	10
11	12	13	14	15
16	17	18	19	20
21	22	23	24	25

DESERVING DE-STRESSING DELIGHT

Clean and Organize

If life feels chaotic around you and out of your control throughout the school year, one of the things you can do to de-stress and give yourself a sense of order and structure is to organize something. The stability of arranging your environment may help you become grounded and peaceful. Sometimes sorting out papers that have piled up and cleaning an overstuffed drawer or closet can give you a sense of calmness. Some people have found that weeding through their clothes creates a feeling of control by systemizing their belongings. The act of organizing can bring you comfort and is a mindless activity that can be useful. Some people may like to rearrange the furniture in a room, wash their car, or scrub their home from top to bottom. Other individuals find planning an event or scheduling their weekly routine brings steadiness and tranquility to their life. These simple acts can help you to be in control and make you feel better when it is over. Completing a task can be an extremely rewarding feat for numerous teachers and support staff. By allowing the time to organize something, educators can feel a sense of achievement and tangible accomplishment. By actually taking a physical action, they feel as if they are contributing to the space around them. Many say that it gives them a greater sense of safety and familiarity that is obtainable and practical. So, go ahead and get organized!

Journal your reaction to this Deserving De-Stressing Delight.

GAME

Crossword Puzzle

HELPFUL HINT-These abbreviations, words, and terms from the vocabulary and bonus lists are missing in the Crossword Puzzle: bottom surgery, compersion, families, FTF, gender diverse, gender dysphoria, gender identity, GSA, intersectionality, MTM, parents, questioning, tracheal shave, trans-identified, and transgender.

ACROSS

2 An 8-letter word that means someone who experiences themselves as both masculine and feminine.

4 An 11-letter word that means a type of relationship where a person is sexually and/or romantically involved with more than one person at the same time.

5 A 4-letter abbreviation that stands for Transgender and Gender Non-Conforming, also described as Transgender/Gender Non-Conforming.

6 An 11-letter word that means a gender that is not exclusively masculine or exclusively feminine and is outside the gender binary.

8 An 11-letter word that means the bottom surgery that involves the removal of testicles.

11 An 8-letter word that means a person who is attracted to both masculine and feminine people.

12 A 16-letter term that means the manner in which a person demonstrates their masculinity and/or femininity that can include clothing, body, behavior, speech, gestures, and other forms of appearance.

15 A 10-letter word that means a mental health or medical professional who controls access to medical treatment such as hormones and surgery.

16 A 7-letter word that means the ability for a person to be read as their affirmed gender by those who are unaware that the individual's identity is transgender.

17 A 5-letter word that means an inclusive umbrella term for all those who identify on the transgender spectrum.

18 A 23-letter term that means the practice of using or referring to a person in the way an individual needs to be addressed, also known as proper gender pronouns.

21 A 15-letter term that means a medicine that blocks the hormone GnRH (Gonadotropin Releasing Hormone).

22 A 12-letter term that means the legal designation of one's gender on official documentation or records.

25 A 10-letter word that means a type of relationship where a person is sexually and/or romantically involved with only one person at a time.

26 A 9-letter word that means someone who is attracted to people of various genders.

27 A 9-letter word that means a gender that is not exclusively male or exclusively female and is outside the gender binary.

28 An 11-letter term that means a gender identity and expression that encompasses a variety of aspects related to femininity and masculinity that could change over time.

29 A 4-letter word that means enacting gender for the purpose of performance or show.

31 An 11-letter word that means someone who possesses both masculine and feminine characteristics.

32 An 8-letter word that means a disdain, hatred, or mistrust of all people female and feminine.

35 An 8-letter word that means a term that describes the name assigned to a person at birth, which they no longer use, for it does not align with their affirmed gender and can also be referred to as their old name.

36 An 8-letter word that means a group of medical conditions where someone can be born with ambiguous genitalia and/or internal sex organs or chromosomal differences that are not clearly male or female.

38 A 13-letter word coined by Julia Serano to describe a form of misogyny that is focused towards trans women.

39 A 4-letter abbreviation that stands for Transgender and Non-Binary or Transgender and Gender Non-Binary, also described as Transgender/Non-Binary.

41 A 9-letter word that means the pattern of thoughts, feelings, and arousal that determine sexual preferences.

44 A 6-letter word that means how a person internally experiences themselves as male, female, masculine, feminine, some combination of these, or none of them; aspects of these can be culturally defined.

45 An 11-letter word that means a person who identifies within the gender binary (either male or female) and may have medical procedures to bring their body in line with their identity. However, not all people who have medical transitions identify as this word.

46 A 4-letter abbreviation that stands for an individual who was assigned male at birth by a medical doctor based on the visible appearance of their genitalia at birth.

47 An 18-letter term that means the advantages granted by society to people whose gender aligns with the gender assigned at birth.

49 A 25-letter term that means a variety of plastic surgery procedures to create a more feminine appearance to the features of the face.

51 A 4-letter abbreviation that stands for an individual who was assigned female at birth by a medical doctor based on the visible appearance of their genitalia at birth.

52 A 10-letter term that means a surgical procedure made to create a masculine-appearing chest or to have breast implants.

53 A 12-letter word that means a type of bottom surgery that entails the construction of a penis and can include the construction of testicles and the implant of an erection device.

54 A 7-letter word that is used for a transgender person who chooses to keep their trans status private.

56 A 12-letter word that means a surgical procedure that creates a scrotal sac and can include testicular implants.

58 A 3-letter word that can designate a number of sexual orientations and possibilities that are not mutually exclusive and may also refer to someone assigned female at birth but who does not identify as, or only partially identifies as, a girl or woman; moreover, they often identify as lesbians, dykes, or queer.

59 A 22-letter term that means surgery that brings the individual's body into alignment with their gender identity.

61 A 5-letter word that refers to a sexual orientation that is not heterosexual and/or anything that is non-heteronormative.

62 A 14-letter word that means a gender-affirming bottom surgery which releases the micro phallus and can include urethra lengthening.

DOWN

1 A 15-letter term that means a type of bottom surgery that usually includes removing the uterus, ovaries, and fallopian tubes and which could involve the removal of the cervix.

2 A 7-letter word that means a practice of using material or clothing to constrict the breasts that enables a person to flatten their chest.

3 A 7-letter word that means the use of prosthetics and/or other materials to enable an individual to possess the appearance and feeling of having a penis and testicles.

5 An 11-letter overarching word which can be used for people whose gender expression and/or gender identity does not align with their sex assigned at birth.

7 An 11-letter word that means the act of a person who is attempting to figure out their own sexuality and/or gender.

9 A 7-letter word that means someone who does not identify with any gender.

10 A 3-letter abbreviation that stands for a Person/People of Color.

12 A 3-letter abbreviation that stands for Gender and Sexualities Alliance, Gay-Straight Alliance, or Gender and Sexuality Alliance and is a school club for students to meet, organize, and educate around issues pertaining to gender and sexuality.

13 A 19-letter term that means a surgical procedure that removes breast tissue from both sides of the chest and can include the construction of a male-appearing chest.

14 A 3-letter abbreviation that means a person who now identifies as female gendered but was assigned a male gender at birth.

19 A 6-letter word that means the act of disclosing someone's sexuality and/or gender identity without their knowledge and/or permission.

20 An 11-letter word that means prejudice, fear, disdain, or discrimination in respect of gender non-conforming and transgender people.

22 A 19-letter term that means people who do not meet common gender norms.

23 A 6-letter word that means the belief that there are only two genders: male and female.

24 A 13-letter word that means the social and/or medical actions a person takes to explore and/or affirm their gender identity.

30 A 12-letter word that means the surgical construction of a vagina.

31 A 7-letter word that means someone who does not feel sexual attraction to other people.

33 A 7-letter word that means a person who is in a sexual and/or romantic relationship with someone.

34 A 4-letter abbreviation which stands for Gonadotropin Releasing Hormone and means a medical term for the hormone that is released by the hypothalamus governing the production of LH (Luteinizing Hormone) and FSH (Follicle-Stimulating Hormone) by the pituitary gland, which causes the gonads to produce estrogen and testosterone.

37 A 15-letter word that means a medical doctor who specializes in glands and hormones.

40 A 9-letter word that means an Indigenous North American identity embraced by some individuals who incorporate a variety of gender roles, identities, and expressions by embodying both masculine and feminine spirits and traits.

42 A 13-letter term that means a surgical procedure that reduces the thyroid cartilage, which makes up the Adam's apple.

43 A 12-letter term that means a system to classify the development of puberty in children.

48 A 6-letter word that means a prescribed routine post-vaginoplasty where a person inserts medical equipment into the neovagina in order to maintain the creation of the vaginal canal.

50 A 9-letter word that means someone whose gender assigned at birth and gender identity are aligned.

55 A 5-letter abbreviation which stands for lesbian, gay, bisexual, transgender, and queer, and/or questioning.

57 A 4-letter word that may also be used as a gender-neutral pronoun to describe a single individual.

60 A 3-letter abbreviation that means a person who now identifies as male gendered but was assigned a female gender at birth.

GRAPHICS GALORE

T-Chart

Document different ways you can adjust your teaching and classroom practices in regard to lessons in all subject areas in order to acknowledge the presence of your TGNB and/or gender questioning students. This graphic organizer can help you understand ways you are comfortable and can easily incorporate methods that are welcoming and inclusive to the needs of your TGNB and/or gender questioning students. It is suggested that you make copies of this graphic prior to its use, in order for you to have the original available at another time.

SUBJECT AREA AND TOPIC:			
1. What lesson do you use now?	2. How can you make it more trans appropriate?	3. What questions will you ask?	4. What materials will you need, including literature?

SAMPLER SHARE

I am submitting my own reply to the *Reflective Responses* question listed below as a sample, hoping to inspire you to use it as a springboard to formulate your own practices. Please be aware that all of the students' names have been removed, as well as most of the actual pronouns for the student and parent, in order to respect the privacy of TGNB and/or gender questioning students, their parents, and other family members. It should be noted that all of these methods can be beneficial for all students, not only those who identify as TGNB and/or are questioning their gender. It is imperative to understand that even without intending to, gender-based practices can negatively impact the social and emotional well-being of students who identify on the transgender spectrum. For these reasons and the need to be transparent, samples are incorporated that portray how the lives of gender-diverse students were also affected, though they did not identify themselves as TGNB and/or gender questioning at the time of the event. Whether they do now, or not, is unknown.

What aspects of the current literature and materials being used in your classroom do you now recognize require adjustments in order to address the needs, inclusion, and acceptance of TGNB and/or gender questioning students?

Something that became extremely apparent to me as my advocacy for TGNB and/or gender questioning students grew was the lack of literature in my classroom and the school library that supported the journeys of students as they navigated their gender. When one of the students I taught began their gender transition and was ready for their four and five-year-old classmates to know, I came across an age-appropriate book to read to my students and began a conversation. I was unsure how the discussion of gender would unfold and what these young students would understand. Using literature as the springboard tool to open an honest dialogue, I found that these young minds grasped the total message quicker than many an adult and with absolutely no negativity. They all shared, in their own age-appropriate way, about how they liked to play with things that people say they should not. They elaborated how friends, parents, siblings, cousins, and other relatives sometimes made fun of them for clothes they preferred to wear, games they wanted to learn, and gifts they asked to get for certain celebrations. They also spoke of how this made them feel and so their seemingly innate sense of understanding and empathy extended to the student who did not identify with their gender assigned at birth. Our community verbal exchanges did not end there. I would read traditional literature, but change specific character names and pronouns, and then pose questions asking them to shape their own thoughts about gender. The questions and conversations with these four to five-year-old students were never-ending, rich, and respectful. It proved to me that gender bias is not an innate state of mind, but rather something that is taught. As an educator, I knew that I could not perpetuate any message that was based on gender bias. For all the years to follow, I chose to be part of the solution and encouraged students to think for themselves when the topic of gender arose in my classroom, anywhere within the school setting, or in society at large.

GRAPHICS GALORE

Timeline

Now that specific adjustments have been made to some of the current lessons you teach in school, it is necessary to reflect on the effectiveness of these changes. As with all lessons that educators implement, it is a common professional practice to review what went well and what still can be improved, when modifying the curriculum to best serve the needs of all students.

TOPIC AND NAME OF LESSON:

What did you try?	What went well and why?	What still needs to be changed and why?	What revised changes will you implement when instructing this lesson again?
Date:	Date:	Date:	Date:

TOPIC AND NAME OF LESSON:

What did you try?	What went well and why?	What still needs to be changed and why?	What revised changes will you implement when instructing this lesson again?
Date:	Date:	Date:	Date:

ANECDOTAL AFFIRMATION

ANECDOTAL AFFIRMATION

Ask not only
What you
Can do for
Your child's school,
But also ask
What their school
Can do for
Your child!

This Anecdotal Affirmation is meant to inspire, provoke thought, and empower your learning in any way that opens your heart. Its presence is intended to set the tone and intention of the chapter. This affirmation may be used as a springboard for writing or as a conversation starter with someone else. Ample space has been provided for you to reflect on the Anecdotal Affirmation.

COMMUNICATION CORNER

Reflecting on your own thoughts and experiences is critical when processing new information and adjusting your thinking. Equally important can be sharing and learning how others analyze their own thoughts and experiences. This exercise was designed with the intention of offering teachers, support staff, and administrators a safe place to discuss all the topics addressed in this chapter. When two or more school employees candidly begin a conversation that embraces an open dialogue without judgment or criticism of one another's beliefs and ideas concerning students and school policies, everyone benefits. It is suggested that after teachers, support staff, and administrators privately answer the questions from the Reflective Responses section, they converse about one or two of them, while others may prefer to answer them all with a trusted colleague or administrator. In order to recall the questions you answered, simply highlight or circle the ones you addressed and then ask others the ones they responded to on their own. By doing so in a respectful and communicative manner that honors the voices of all those working or interacting with the students who identify as transgender, non-binary, and/or are questioning their gender, teachers, support staff, and administrators in your school can positively impact the lives of the students they are committed to serve as professionals. Do you and your colleague or administrator answer these questions in the same way or differently? Discuss your responses to understand how all of you view the answers to the questions and make time to celebrate all you learn from being willing to communicate with one another.

1. What aspects of your practices being used in your classroom specifically address the needs, inclusion, and acceptance of TGNB and/or gender questioning students?

    . . . .

    . . . .

2. What aspects of the practices being used throughout the school specifically address the needs, inclusion, and acceptance of TGNB and/or gender questioning students?

    . . . .

    . . . .

3. What aspects of the current curriculum and lesson plans being used in your classroom specifically address the needs, inclusion, and acceptance of TGNB and/or gender questioning students?

. . . .

. . . .

4. What aspects of the current curriculum and lesson plans being used throughout the school specifically address the needs, inclusion, and acceptance of TGNB and/or gender questioning students?

. . . .

. . . .

5. What aspects of the current curriculum and lesson plans being used in your classroom do you now recognize require adjustments in order to address the needs, inclusion, and acceptance of TGNB and/or gender questioning students?

. . . .

. . . .

6. What aspects of the current curriculum and lesson plans being used throughout the school do you now recognize require adjustments in order to address the needs, inclusion, and acceptance of TGNB and/or gender questioning students?

. . . .

. . . .

7. What aspects of the current literature and materials being used in your classroom do you now recognize require adjustments in order to address the needs, inclusion, and acceptance of TGNB and/or gender questioning students?

. . . .

. . . .

8. What aspects of the current literature and materials being used throughout the school do you now recognize require adjustments in order to address the needs, inclusion, and acceptance of TGNB and/or gender questioning students?

. . . .

. . . .

9. How has the intersectionality of your identities influenced your interactions and educational practices in the classroom with TGNB and/or gender questioning students?

. . . .

. . . .

10. What can you and your colleagues do to ensure the needs, inclusion, and acceptance of the TGNB and/or gender questioning students in your classroom and/or school?

. . . .

. . . .

11. What do you feel administrators can do to ensure the needs, inclusion, and acceptance of the TGNB and/or gender questioning students in your classroom and/or school?

. . . .

. . . .

12. What do you feel the student body can do to ensure the needs, inclusion, and acceptance of the TGNB and/or gender questioning students in your classroom and/or school?

. . . .

. . . .

Chapter 7

CELEBRATING THE CHANGES AND PASSING ON THE MESSAGE

VITAL VIGNETTE

Congratulations! This chapter is all about celebrating the paradigm shifts, sincere attempts, and all that you have accomplished as an educator. How often has it been said that change takes time? Nothing happens overnight in most professional fields and this is also true in education. However, it is important to acknowledge when growth does occur. It is heartening to watch the motivational drive of teachers, support staff, and other school personnel as they strive to improve the lives of each student, as well as help them reach their true potential in becoming whole and ready to face the world with pride and optimism. It is vital to always remember that TGNB students and their families look up to and count on those working in school settings. You may be their only or first ally, for school personnel are the front line! With this privileged responsibility comes the need to be educated. Fortunately, it is still the assigned role of the school to provide the opportunity for learning by offering continuous training. By agreeing to participate in the readings, exercises, games, and conversations presented in this resource, you are now armed with the tools required to support TGNB and/or gender questioning students. What have you learned by engaging in this process?

It is necessary to recognize and celebrate your own educational transition, as well as that of your school. Acknowledging your willingness to empower TGNB students and/or those who are questioning their gender is extremely praiseworthy. The steps you will now need to ensure the acquired changes and build on what was already in place will guarantee the deserving safety and well-being of all students who identify on the transition spectrum and/or are questioning their gender. If administrators notice that there are still teachers and support staff not comfortable accepting the needs of TGNB and/or gender questioning students in school, it will be essential to figure out which teachers and staff are eager to learn how to support these students and begin with them. Carrying this torch may not always be easy and sometimes it will seem like an uphill battle. Nonetheless, that will make it all the more rewarding when positive outcomes are achieved.

To teacher and support staff advocates, your voice and expertise will be called on to use the knowledge you have absorbed from using this workbook that enabled you to participate in this worthwhile and meaningful journey. What you have gained can prove to be monumental. As a result of being trained and open to learning the information in this interactive resource, all school personnel will now be familiar with once-unknown vocabulary and have the answers to questions and concerns that at one point in time may have been baffling. While guiding the school population, you are equipped to assist in the writing and implementation of respectful policies affecting the welfare of TGNB and/or gender questioning students.

You are now aware that though gender and sexuality are connected, particularly when discussing dating, they are notably distinct from each other. Being in the know, you now comprehend that students who identify on the transgender spectrum can also include an individual who identifies on the autism spectrum and/or has special needs. Moreover, specific assumptions may not be entirely true, such as believing that if someone identifies as LGBTQQIA+, this automatically qualifies them as the most knowledgeable, the best ambassador, the ultimate advocate, or the only choice to defend trans students. In contrast, it is not necessarily correct to presuppose that if an individual is part of a religious group, or is of a certain culture, they will be unsupportive of the Trans community.

After obtaining information from this workbook, you have gained the expertise of knowing the distinctions between a social and a medical transition. Schools will have an ethical, and when applicable, legal obligation to respect aspects of the social transition: name and pronoun changes, manners of dress, padding and hairstyles, physical movements and gestures, voice adjustment, etc. Furthermore, if medical interventions are part of a minor's transition, there should be a clear understanding that most often it will be in the form of puberty blockers or gender-affirming hormones. In addition, school personnel will now be cognizant that many TGNB and/or gender questioning students are combating gender dysphoria and therefore socially and/or medically transitioning will be their primary means to alleviate it. In connection with factors related to social transition, committees and individuals establishing policies must be alerted to the importance of ensuring that all computer logins and school files use the TGNB student's affirmed name, pronoun, and gender marker. At this point, there should be no doubt among all school staff that confidentiality and the wishes of TGNB students and their families must be paramount while assuring them protection, vowing to abide by laws, and committing to create school policies that will better their school lives.

As you actively engage with the parents of students who identify on the transgender spectrum, it is significant to keep in mind that though they may be acting on their child's behalf, some parents can still be navigating the transition for themselves which may involve varying stages of grief. This process can include the possible mourning attached to saying goodbye to specific aspects of their child's gender assigned at birth. In some instances, parents might feel a loss should they be rejected by family, friends, or certain communities. Many family members will experience an outpouring of encouragement and loyalty, where others may be judged and berated for supporting their child. As a part of the school community, you have the opportunity to provide stability and assistance to parents, as well as to their TGNB and/or gender questioning child.

It would be extremely valuable for these students if policy makers incorporate guidelines that align with the needs and wishes of TGNB students and their families in relation to safety, with emphasis on bathrooms, locker rooms, bullying, and harassment. Likewise, it is necessary to explain that those in charge of designing school policies must address issues associated with team sports and comprehend how transitioning can affect these students' participation on teams and college scholarships. Furthermore, it is vital to generate policies that encourage and welcome TGNB and/or gender questioning students to partake in all school clubs, activities, and events in order to promote a school culture that will set a tone that fosters inclusion and acceptance.

To declare that accurate training, focusing on trans issues, school policies, and laws for all those who work with TGNB and/or gender questioning students is imperative would be quite an understatement. If the individual or those who are leading the training do not know the answer to a question, current law, or up-to-date policy, it is their responsibility to ask, research, and acquire the information, for nothing should be guessed or assumed. Here, more than ever, facts matter and their accuracy will affect the lives of TGNB and/or gender questioning students. For continuity and with the parents' permission, only on a need-to-know basis, the following year's teacher/s and all related school personnel should confidentially be informed of a student's gender transition. As this book illustrates in detail, every individual who interacts with or is involved in an action that affects students must be educated and trained on issues and rights affecting TGNB and/or gender questioning students.

Once all school personnel, volunteers, and others employed by your school are properly trained, the process of updating school policies and being aware of current laws will also be required. As new students and recently hired staff join your school, they too must receive the same information and guidance that is consistent with previous training. This is also relevant for volunteers and substitutes. If training cannot occur immediately, and only as a temporary solution, schools may provide a detailed document to those who will be trained in the very near future which states the essential rights and school policies that protect TGNB students and/or those who are questioning their gender.

It is critical to understand and know that for some students gender may be fluid and evolving on a daily basis. It is key to have an ongoing and open dialogue with all students that welcomes them to engage in private conversations to express their needs. Constructing solutions together that preserve the dignity of TGNB and/or gender questioning students enables schools to create policies that address and reflect these challenges. However, this is not to dismiss that the gender binary exists for the majority of students and is always present. Nevertheless, carving out positive, visible, and verbal experiences in schools for those who do identify on the transgender spectrum is crucial and can be a lifeline for many students. Integrating inclusive, safe spaces within the curriculum and literature, and providing resources for those students who identify as TGNB and/or gender questioning, alongside those who identify on the gender binary, is important. The hope is that all those in the field of education join in accepting TGNB students and/or those who are questioning their gender. The more educated all teachers, support staff, administrators, and community members are in relation to the needs and rights of these students, the better we can support their journeys. Thanks to your involvement and commitment to this profession, the future of education will continue embracing and celebrating our similarities and differences, as well as positively impacting school culture. As we all honor the same desire to be treated with dignity and the respect we deserve, always remember, this includes our TGNB and/or gender questioning students, too!

ANECDOTAL AFFIRMATION

ANECDOTAL
AFFIRMATION

Let kindness
Fill our hearts,
Let support
Fill our actions,
Let protection
Fill our policies,
Let acceptance
Fill our school
days.

This Anecdotal Affirmation is meant to inspire, provoke thought, and empower your learning in any way that opens your heart. Its presence is intended to set the tone and intention of the chapter. This affirmation may be used as a springboard for writing or as a conversation starter with someone else. Ample space has been provided for you to reflect on the Anecdotal Affirmation.

GRAPHICS GALORE

Splash

Can you jot down all those who should be celebrated in your school as a result of this learning process in reference to your school and students' transition? As you brainstorm, write the names of those who should be celebrated by quickly and randomly scattering them anywhere on the page in a splash-like manner. Use the information obtained from the *Splash* to assess those you already recognize should be celebrated in relation to supporting the learning process, as your school and students transition.

REFLECTIVE RESPONSES

1. In what ways have you shifted your way of thinking to specifically address the needs, inclusion, and acceptance of TGNB and/or gender questioning students?

....

....

....

....

....

....

....

....

2. In what ways have you noticed that your colleagues have shifted their way of thinking to specifically address the needs, inclusion, and acceptance of TGNB and/or gender questioning students?

....

....

....

....

....

....

....

3. In what ways have you noticed that your administrators have shifted their way of thinking to specifically address the needs, inclusion, and acceptance of TGNB and/or gender questioning students?

4. In what ways have you noticed that students have shifted their way of thinking to specifically address the needs, inclusion, and acceptance of TGNB and/or gender questioning students?

5. In what ways have you shifted your educational practices to specifically address the needs, inclusion, and acceptance of TGNB and/or gender questioning students?

6. In what ways have your colleagues shifted their educational practices to specifically address the needs, inclusion, and acceptance of TGNB and/or gender questioning students?

7. In what ways have you noticed that school policies have shifted to specifically address the needs, inclusion, and acceptance of TGNB and/or gender questioning students in relation to bathroom and locker room use?

....

....

....

....

....

....

....

8. In what ways have you noticed that school policies have shifted to specifically address the needs, inclusion, and acceptance of TGNB and/or gender questioning students in relation to participation in team sports, membership in clubs, and involvement in school activities and events?

....

....

....

....

....

....

....

9. In what ways have you noticed that school policies have shifted to specifically address the needs, inclusion, and acceptance of TGNB and/or gender questioning students in relation to the way bullying and harassment in school are managed?

....

....

....

....

....

....

....

....

10. In what ways have you noticed that parents, guardians, caregivers, and family members have shifted their thinking to specifically address the needs, inclusion, and acceptance of TGNB and/or gender questioning students in relation to bullying and harassment, bathroom and locker room use, and policies regarding team sports, clubs, activities, and events in school?

....

....

....

....

....

....

....

11. In what ways have you noticed that other community members have shifted their thinking to specifically address the needs, inclusion, and acceptance of TGNB and/or gender questioning students in relation to bullying and harassment, bathroom and locker room use, and policies regarding team sports, clubs, activities, and events in school?

12. In what ways and areas do you feel there is still a necessity for some, perhaps much, growth in awareness and sensitivity for those who have contact with TGNB and/or gender questioning students in your school, in order to specifically address their needs, inclusion, and acceptance? What can you do to help make that positive difference?

GAME

Matching Pre-Test 6

It is important to be aware of what you know and to use that knowledge as a starting point to grow. After taking the pre-test, you will realize what you still need to learn. The tools in this chapter were created to help you internalize the vocabulary. As a pre-test, match the vocabulary (the numbers) with the definitions (the letters) by drawing a line from a number to a letter. Each number and letter should only be used once. What were your results? The answer keys are provided in the Answer Key section in Chapter 8. It is suggested that you check your answers after you have taken the pre-test to see how well you did. Feel free to repeat this process at a later time; you may choose to use this activity to assess your progress by using this game as a post-test.

1. TGNB	A. A word that may be used as a gender-neutral pronoun to describe a single individual.
2. TGNC	B. An abbreviation that stands for Transgender and Non-Binary or Transgender and Gender Non-Binary, also described as Transgender/Non-Binary.
3. they	C. An overarching word which can be used for people whose gender expression and/or gender identity does not align with their sex assigned at birth.
4. top surgery	D. A word coined by Julia Serano to describe a form of misogyny that is focused towards trans women.
5. tracheal shave	E. The surgical construction of a vagina.
6. transgender/ trans-identified	F. An abbreviation that stands for Transgender and Gender Non-Conforming, also described as Transgender/Gender Non-Conforming.
7. transitioning	G. A surgical procedure made to create a masculine-appearing chest or to have breast implants.
8. transmisogyny	H. An Indigenous North American identity embraced by some individuals who incorporate a variety of gender roles, identities, and expressions by embodying both masculine and feminine spirits and traits.
9. transphobia	I. The social and/or medical actions a person takes to explore and/or affirm their gender identity.
10. transsexual	J. Prejudice, fear, disdain, or discrimination in respect of gender non-conforming and transgender people.
11. two-spirit	K. A surgical procedure that reduces the thyroid cartilage, which makes up the Adam's apple.
12. vaginoplasty	L. A person who identifies within the gender binary (either male or female) and may have medical procedures to bring their body in line with their identity. However, not all people who have medical transitions identify as this word.

Retake this pre-test as a post-test to assess your personal progress and knowledge.

EMPATHY-EMBRACING EXERCISE

Whether all teachers, support staff, and administrators support the transition process or not, there will most likely be at least one aspect worth celebrating. For those teachers, support staff, and administrators who are supportive, the celebrations will probably be many throughout the student's transition. It is important to recognize and even document these moments of growth. For those who are not supportive, it may take much inner strength to accept a student's transition. If you take the time to reflect, most likely there will be something that you learned about yourself, your student/s, and/or others who serve students in a school setting in relation to the transition. This question asks you to ponder and celebrate the positive.

Has there been a time in your life when you did something you dreamed of or needed to do for yourself which felt worthy of celebrating and may have had a major effect or impact on another person's life and/or core beliefs? If so, what was it? How, if at all, did it affect your and their life?

GRAPHICS GALORE

Venn Diagram

List the lessons and/or policies you and a colleague each implement now to support TGNB students. Once this is completed, then record the lessons and/or policies that overlap for both you and a colleague. Please note, it is extremely important to celebrate all you have learned and understand that as more policies and/or lessons are implemented in school, which support those who identify as TGNB and/or gender questioning, the greater positive impact they will have on these students' lives both in and out of school.

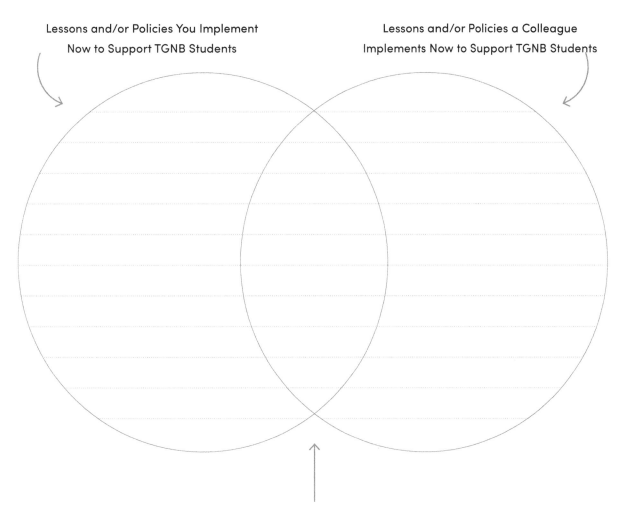

Lessons and/or Policies You Implement
Now to Support TGNB Students

Lessons and/or Policies a Colleague
Implements Now to Support TGNB Students

Overlapping Lessons and/or Policies You and a
Colleague Implement Now to Support TGNB Students

DESERVING DE-STRESSING DELIGHT

Pamper, Nurture, and Self-Care

What can be more loving than nurturing and pampering your body and soul? As educators and support staff who are always there for others, you must embrace your own self-care because it is essential for your personal health and emotional well-being. Pampering can be experienced in a multitude of ways and often finances can dictate the type of things you can afford. For some, a massage can be the most calming and rejuvenating form of self-care. When low on funds, massage schools may offer services at a nominal fee or no cost when done by a trainee who needs to practice their skills. Another possibility is going to a nail salon and having an inexpensive ten-minute chair massage. Sometimes, requesting gift cards for holidays and special occasions and using those funds for a luxury massage can do the trick, too.

Other ways people indulge in the nurturing of their body include having their hair cut and/or dyed, getting their nails done, or purchasing moisturizing creams and having someone they adore apply it on them. There are days that family members allow themselves to sleep longer or take a nap in the middle of the day. Some people find it liberating to dress up and go out to eat in a fancy restaurant with a family member, close friend, or simply by themselves. Included in self-care is giving yourself permission to shop, especially for clothing. Treating yourself with a special gift that is within your budget will remind you that you have value and worth.

One individual found being around dogs very comforting, but they did not own a dog, so they offered to dog-sit for friends, free of charge. Taking care of your body by exercising can be extremely nurturing and a healthy expression of self-care. Another person enjoyed cooking. They would take the ingredients they had in their home and challenge themselves to make a meal using only the components that were available. Many people have found free and thrifty ways to practice self-care by going for a meditative bicycle ride in their neighborhood, using a free-pass coupon to a gym, and taking a free, open yoga class when special promotions are advertised.

Caring for your own needs and focusing on your own body and soul are some of the kindest and most respectful ways a person who works with students can honor themselves. As you journey through this process of absorbing new policies and procedures in relation to your students, it is critical to learn how to satisfy your personal desires. Lovingly pampering, nurturing, and caring for your own body must be at the top of the list!

Journal your reaction to this Deserving De-Stressing Delight.

. . . .

. . . .

. . . .

GAME

Untangle-n-Spell

This game can be played alone or as a race against other players. The letters on the left side of every row are the mixed-up version of the correct spelling of an actual word, term, or abbreviation from the vocabulary or bonus list created for this workbook. The word, term, or abbreviation needs to be untangled and written onto the right side of the game sheet below. If this game is played as a race, the player who completes the game first must verbally state the word "Untangle," and all players must stop writing. Then another player should check the answers against the answer key for both the correct spelling of the words, terms, and abbreviations to confirm their presence on either the vocabulary or bonus list. If the player has not accurately completed both criteria, they are disqualified and the other players need to have their sheet checked using the same guidelines. Whichever player has the most correct answers, at the time that the original player stops the game, becomes the winner. An alternative way to play this game is to have all players agree to an amount of time to play the game, then set a timer for that time frame, and stop the game once the allotted time is over. If a player finishes the game before the time is up, players must follow the directions stated above. If the game is over after the time is over, whichever player has the most correct answers, according to both pieces of criteria, becomes the winner. (HINT: The 15 words, terms, and abbreviations used in this game were not used in the Crossword Puzzle offered in the last chapter of this workbook.) The Answer Key is in Chapter 8. Please note: numbers 4, 7, 8, 11, 12, and 14 will actually create two words from the letters provided.

UNTANGLE-N-SPELL	
1. t e y i t n s i r c l a i e t n o	_ _ _ _ _ _ _ _ _ _ _ _ _ _ _ _
2. o n p c s o m i r e	_ _ _ _ _ _ _ _ _
3. s l e m a i f i	_ _ _ _ _ _ _
4. n g d r e e e e i v d r s	_ _ _ _ _ _ _ _ _ _ _
5. A S G	_ _ _
6. g a n r e n t r e s d	_ _ _ _ _ _ _ _ _ _
7. d e n e r g i t n i y e t d	_ _ _ _ _ _ _ _ _ _ _ _
8. t m o t o b r g u e y s r	_ _ _ _ _ _ _ _ _ _ _
9. T M M	_ _ _
10. i q n t g s u n i o e	_ _ _ _ _ _ _ _ _ _
11. c l a r e t a h v s e h a	_ _ _ _ _ _ _ _ _ _ _
12. r n a s t e d n i i t e f d i	_ _ _ _ _ _ _ _ _ _ _ _ _
13. a t e p s r n	_ _ _ _ _ _
14. e g r e n d y a p d i s o h r	_ _ _ _ _ _ _ _ _ _ _ _
15. FFT	_ _ _

GRAPHICS GALORE

Box

Adjusting educational practices and incorporating policy directives is not always easy to do. In addition, learning about or implementing new and unfamiliar school guidelines can take a great deal of effort. All of these endeavors are something that deserve to be celebrated. List any educational practices, policy directives, and use of new and unfamiliar school guidelines that others learned or did that should be celebrated. Whenever applicable, include the name of the individual/s who instituted this practice or directive.

1	2	3	4	5
6	7	8	9	10
11	12	13	14	15
16	17	18	19	20
21	22	23	24	25

SAMPLER SHARE

I am submitting my own reply to the *Reflective Responses* question listed below as a sample, hoping to inspire you to use it as a springboard to formulate your own practices. Please be aware that all of the students' names have been removed, as well as most of the actual pronouns for the student and parent, in order to respect the privacy of TGNB and/or gender questioning students, their parents, and other family members. It should be noted that all of these methods can be beneficial for all students, not only those who identify as TGNB and/or are questioning their gender. It is imperative to understand that even without intending to, gender-based practices can negatively impact the social and emotional well-being of students who identify on the transgender spectrum. For these reasons and the need to be transparent, samples are incorporated that portray how the lives of gender-diverse students were also affected, though they did not identify themselves as TGNB and/or gender questioning at the time of the event. Whether they do now, or not, is unknown.

In what ways have you noticed that students have shifted their way of thinking to specifically address the needs, inclusion, and acceptance of TGNB and/or gender questioning students?

As I walked the halls in my school, it became evident that teachers, support staff, administrators, and community members were understanding the importance of rethinking and reeducating themselves to learn about the needs and rights of TGNB and/or gender questioning students. The boy/girl graphs were fewer, the students were asked which pronoun and/or name they use, and several classrooms displayed some form of literature that enabled TGNB and/or gender questioning students to see themselves in the characters. Moreover, I overheard teachers allowing students to select any gift they chose out of the reward box. Many substitute plans included the way a TGNB and/or gender questioning student wanted to be addressed, even if it was different from the name on their legal documents. Furthermore, I was informed that TGNB and/or gender questioning students created videos for social media that shared their personal stories and were then publicly honored by their peers and school personnel. In addition, teachers and support staff alike reported that parents were feeling safe enough to discuss their child's gender questioning and request guidance in the form of resources and counseling assistance.

Yet of all the growth I observed, the single most memorable moment was when I began working in a different school within the school district and a second grader, whom I had never taught, approached me by name in the hall and requested to speak with me for a minute. When I stopped to listen, she told me that she remembered I had been the teacher of a particular student and told me the student's name. She then continued, with much kindness and urgency, that I needed to be aware that if I saw that student in this school, I should no longer call them by the name I did when I taught them. This young person told me to only call this student by a name she announced to me was their name now. She added that I should never say "she" anymore when I talked about the student, only "he." The second grader ended by asking me if I understood and I quickly told her I did. I thanked her for the update and she smiled. When this compassionate second grader walked away, I moved to the corner of the hallway and cried, not out of sadness, but of absolute awe and hope, knowing that if a young student could learn and accept TGNB and/or gender questioning students so easily, so could all those who chose to educate students in a school setting!

GRAPHICS GALORE

Pie Graph

Decide how significant these topics are to you in relation to each other. Place the number that corresponds with a suggested topic within as many slices of the pie that conveys how each one matters to you. Only one number should be placed in each slice. You do not need to use all the topics, but do fill in all the slices. Feel free to create your own topics and assign them their own number. It is critical that educators process and reflect on their feelings about these crucial policies that will continue to affect the lives of students who identify as TGNB and/or are questioning their gender. More importantly, educators must overcome their own possible conflicting beliefs to ensure that they always treat all students with the dignity and respect they deserve.

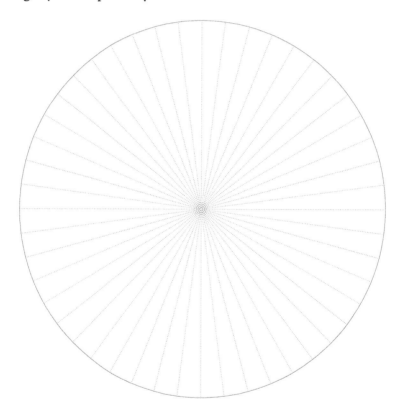

To what degree are these policy concerns and related topics important to you? The policies your school has for protecting the rights and dignity of TGNB and/or gender questioning students...

1. In relation to the bathroom, locker room, and sports.

2. In relation to bullying and/or harassment.

3. In relation to activities, after-school clubs, and/or classes.

4. In relation to implementation of new and updated regulations.

5. In relation to providing current and appropriate resources in a variety of ways.

6. In relation to teacher, support staff, and administrator training.

7. In relation to parent, student, and other school personnel training.

8. In relation to proms, gendered parties, and accommodations for field trips and overnight stays.

9. In relation to dressing room use regarding theater productions and off-site swimming lessons.

10. In relation to creating a curriculum that reflects and validates their existence by incorporating trans history and the use of "they/them/their" as a singular pronoun within all subject areas.

ANECDOTAL AFFIRMATION

ANECDOTAL AFFIRMATION

*Honor your own
Educational transition,
As your school
And students
Transition!*

This Anecdotal Affirmation is meant to inspire, provoke thought, and empower your learning in any way that opens your heart. Its presence is intended to set the tone and intention of the chapter. This affirmation may be used as a springboard for writing or as a conversation starter with someone else. Ample space has been provided for you to reflect on the Anecdotal Affirmation.

COMMUNICATION CORNER

Reflecting on your own thoughts and experiences is critical when processing new information and adjusting your thinking. Equally important can be sharing and learning how others analyze their own thoughts and experiences. This exercise was designed with the intention of offering teachers, support staff, and administrators a safe place to discuss all the topics addressed in this chapter. When two or more school employees candidly begin a conversation that embraces an open dialogue without judgment or criticism of one another's beliefs and ideas concerning students and school policies, everyone benefits. It is suggested that after teachers, support staff, and administrators privately answer the questions from the Reflective Responses section, they converse about one or two of them, while others may prefer to answer them all with a trusted colleague or administrator. In order to recall the questions you answered, simply highlight or circle the ones you addressed and then ask others the ones they responded to on their own. By doing so in a respectful and communicative manner that honors the voices of all those working or interacting with the students who identify as transgender, non-binary, and/or are questioning their gender, teachers, support staff, and administrators in your school can positively impact the lives of the students they are committed to serve as professionals. Do you and your colleague or administrator answer these questions in the same way or differently? Discuss your responses to understand how all of you view the answers to the questions and make time to celebrate all you learn from being willing to communicate with one another.

1. In what ways have you shifted your way of thinking to specifically address the needs, inclusion, and acceptance of TGNB and/or gender questioning students?

. . . .

. . . .

2. In what ways have you noticed that your colleagues have shifted their way of thinking to specifically address the needs, inclusion, and acceptance of TGNB and/or gender questioning students?

. . . .

. . . .

3. In what ways have you noticed that your administrators have shifted their way of thinking to specifically address the needs, inclusion, and acceptance of TGNB and/or gender questioning students?

. . . .

. . . .

4. In what ways have you noticed that students have shifted their way of thinking to specifically address the needs, inclusion, and acceptance of TGNB and/or gender questioning students?

. . . .

. . . .

5. In what ways have you shifted your educational practices to specifically address the needs, inclusion, and acceptance of TGNB and/or gender questioning students?

. . . .

. . . .

6. In what ways have your colleagues shifted their educational practices to specifically address the needs, inclusion, and acceptance of TGNB and/or gender questioning students?

. . . .

. . . .

7. In what ways have you noticed that school policies have shifted to specifically address the needs, inclusion, and acceptance of TGNB and/or gender questioning students in relation to bathroom and locker room use?

. . . .

. . . .

8. In what ways have you noticed that school policies have shifted to specifically address the needs, inclusion, and acceptance of TGNB and/or gender questioning students in relation to participation in team sports, membership in clubs, and involvement in school activities and events?

. . . .

. . . .

9. In what ways have you noticed that school policies have shifted to specifically address the needs, inclusion, and acceptance of TGNB and/or gender questioning students in relation to the way bullying and harassment in school are managed?

. . . .

. . . .

10. In what ways have you noticed that parents, guardians, caregivers, and family members have shifted their thinking to specifically address the needs, inclusion, and acceptance of TGNB and/or gender questioning students in relation to bullying and harassment, bathroom and locker room use, and policies regarding team sports, clubs, activities, and events in school?

. . . .

. . . .

11. In what ways have you noticed that other community members have shifted their thinking to specifically address the needs, inclusion, and acceptance of TGNB and/or gender questioning students in relation to bullying and harassment, bathroom and locker room use, and policies regarding team sports, clubs, activities, and events in school?

. . . .

. . . .

12. In what ways and areas do you feel there is still a necessity for some, perhaps much, growth in awareness and sensitivity for those who have contact with TGNB and/or gender questioning students in your school, in order to specifically address their needs, inclusion, and acceptance? What can you do to help make that positive difference?

. . . .

. . . .

Chapter 8

RESOURCES, ANSWER KEYS, AND GLOSSARY...OH, MY!

VITAL VIGNETTE

If you would like to reach out to the author to share your thoughts and questions in reference to this workbook or to learn more about her workshops, retreats, and speaking engagements, contact D. M. Maynard at: dmmaynardworkbook@gmail.com

I recognize that resources are a crucial aspect of any book, so I am providing you with ones I feel are relevant at the time of writing. Since resources and information are rapidly being updated and changed on a daily basis, some sources or recommendations listed today can be outdated within a month's time. In addition, there may be very valuable resources which could arise while this workbook is in production or are not ones I was familiar with at the time this workbook was created. If any reader knows of any credible resource that was useful to them during their journey and it is not listed below, kindly email me the source. If, after I review the information and am able to confirm that the suggestion aligns with the purpose of this workbook, I would be happy to share it with teachers, support staff, administrators, and other school personnel. That being said, here is the list of resources and I hope you find them useful.

RESOURCES

ARTICLES

Amy Hillier and Elisabeth Torg (2019) "Parent participation in a support group for families with transgender and gender-nonconforming children: Being in the company of others who do not question the reality of our experience." *Transgender Health*, 4(1): 168–175. Published online August 12, 2019. doi: 10.1089/trgh.2018.0018.

Jeff Schwaner (2017) "Understanding These Gender Terms Is Easy." Accessed on May 15, 2018 at www.newsleader.com/story/news/2017/09/20/understanding-these-gender-terms-easy/679663001.

Simon van der Weele (2017) "Mourning Moppa: Mourning without loss in Jill Soloway's *Transparent*." *TSQ: Transgender Studies Quarterly*, 4, (3–4): 608–626.

CHILDREN'S BOOKS

Jennifer Carr (2010) *Be Who You Are* (AuthorHouse).
Nick was born in a boy's body, but has always felt like a girl inside. Nick's family supports him when he says he no longer wants to be called a boy or dress like a boy: "Always remember to be who you are Nick. Remember that we love you, and we are so proud of you" (p.17). Nick's parents find a group for families like theirs. With their support, Nick expresses a desire to be addressed as "she," and then to be named "Hope." Based on the author's experiences with her children.

Jessica Herthel and Jazz Jennings (2014) *I Am Jazz* (Dial Books).
This is the story of a transgender child based on the real-life experience of Jazz Jennings, who has become a spokesperson for trans kids everywhere and now has a television series on TLC. From the time she was two years old, Jazz knew that she had a girl's brain in a boy's body. She loved pink and dressing up as a mermaid and didn't feel like herself in boys' clothing. This confused her family, until they took her to a doctor who said that Jazz was transgender and that she was born that way. Jazz's story tells her story in a simple, clear way that will be appreciated by picture book readers, their parents, and teachers. For information on the television series: www.tlc.com/tv-shows/i-am-jazz.

Colt Keo-Meier (2017) *Stacey's Not a Girl* (Self-Published).
This book takes us on a gender journey with Stacey who does not feel like a girl, but is not so sure they are a boy either. This book introduces us to ideas of gender beyond the binary. It is the first book of its kind with all transgender contributors: author, illustrator, and designer. Elements from each contributor as well as close friends and family are woven into Stacey's story.

Cheryl Kilodavis (2010) *My Princess Boy* (Aladdin).
Dyson loves pink, sparkly things. Sometimes he wears dresses. Sometimes he wears jeans. He likes to wear his princess tiara, even when climbing trees. He's a Princess Boy. This is a story about unconditional love and one remarkable family. Inspired by the author's son, and by her own initial struggles to understand, this heartwarming book is a call for tolerance and an end to bullying and judgments. The world is a brighter place when we accept everyone for who they are.

Kyle Lukoff (2019) *When Aidan Became a Brother* (Lee & Low Books).
When Aidan was born, everyone thought he was a girl. His parents gave him a pretty name, his room looked like a girl's room, and he wore clothes that other girls liked wearing. After he realized he was a trans boy, Aidan and his parents fixed the parts of his life that didn't fit anymore, and now he is settled happily into his new life. Then Mom and Dad announce that they're going to have another baby, and Aidan wants to do everything he can to make things right for his new sibling from the beginning—from choosing the perfect name, to creating a beautiful room, to picking out the cutest onesie. But what does "making things right" actually mean? And what happens if he messes up? With a little help, Aidan comes to understand that mistakes can be fixed with honesty and communication, and that he already knows the most important thing about being a big brother: how to love with his whole self. This heartwarming book will resonate with transgender children, reassure any child concerned about becoming an older sibling, and celebrate the many transitions a family can experience.

Robb Pearlman (2018) *Pink is for Boys* (Running Press Kids).
This is an empowering and educational picture book that proves colors are for everyone, regardless of gender. Pink is for boys...and girls...and everyone! This timely and beautiful book rethinks and reframes the stereotypical blue/pink gender binary and empowers kids and their grown-ups to express themselves in every color of the rainbow. Featuring a diverse group of relatable characters, this book invites and encourages girls and boys to enjoy what they love to do, whether it's racing cars and playing baseball, or loving unicorns and dressing up. Vibrant illustrations help children learn and identify the myriad colors that surround them every day, from the orange of a popsicle, to the green of a grassy field, all the way up to the wonder of a multicolored rainbow. Parents and kids will delight in the author's sweet, simple script, as well as its powerful message: life is not color-coded.

Sarah Savage and Fox Fisher (2017) *Are You a Boy or Are You a Girl?* (Jessica Kingsley Publishers).
Tiny prefers not to tell other children whether they are a boy or girl. Tiny also loves to play fancy dress, sometimes as a fairy and sometimes as a knight in shining armor. Tiny's family don't seem to mind, but when they start a new school some of their new classmates struggle to understand.

Theresa Thorn (2019) *It Feels Good to Be Yourself: A Book About Gender Identity* (Henry Holt & Co).

This picture book introduces the concept of gender identity to the youngest reader. Some people are boys. Some people are girls. Some people are both, neither, or somewhere in between. This sweet, straightforward exploration of gender identity will give children a fuller understanding of themselves and others. With child-friendly language and vibrant art, this book provides young readers and parents alike with the vocabulary to discuss this important topic with sensitivity.

Brook Pessin-Whedbee (2016) *Who Are You? The Kid's Guide to Gender Identity* (Jessica Kingsley Publishers).

This brightly illustrated children's book provides a straightforward introduction to gender for anyone aged five to eight. It presents clear and direct language for understanding and talking about how we experience gender: our bodies, our expression, and our identity. An interactive three-layered wheel included in the book is a simple, yet powerful, tool to clearly demonstrate the difference between our body, how we express ourselves through our clothes and hobbies, and our gender identity. Ideal for use in the classroom or at home, a short page-by-page guide for adults at the back of the book further explains the key concepts and identifies useful discussion points. This is a one-of-a-kind resource for understanding and celebrating the gender diversity that surrounds us.

CAMPS AND CONFERENCES

Camps for LGBTQ Youth Recommended by PFLAG.org

What do you get when you combine s'mores, archery, arts, wilderness skills, and bug juice with a safe space for LGBTQ youth and families? The camps listed on this website all fit the bill according to PFLAG.org, offering the activities you'd find at a traditional summer camp with a safe and nurturing environment for LGBTQ kids.

Please note: This list is offered only as a starting point for those who are searching for a camp that states it supports LGBTQ Youth; however, as with every camp youth attends, it is highly recommended that the organization is thoroughly researched and whenever possible, it is suggested that the camp be visited and/or investigated prior to enrolling a child, in order to ensure the youth's safety and well-being.'
https://pflag.org/youthcamps

Gender Conference NYC—New York, USA

Gender Conference NYC has its roots in Gender Conference East (GCE), which began in 2014 in Baltimore, Maryland. The seed was planted in 2008 when mothers in both Maryland and New York were eager for support and community. They found each other, and with the help of PFLAG Columbia-Howard County, PFLAG NYC, The Ackerman Institute's Gender & Family Project, and Gender Spectrum, Gender Conference East was born. After a move to Newark in 2016, GCE continued to grow. By 2018, the increasing number of

families in need resulted in the founders of GCE creating events in two locations, and Gender Conference NYC was born.
www.genderconference.nyc

Gender Odyssey—San Diego, California and Seattle, Washington, USA

This is an international conference focused on the needs and interests of transgender and gender-diverse children of all ages, their families and supporters, and the professionals who serve them. The conference is packed with thought-provoking workshops, including medical information and consultation opportunities, professional education, discussion groups, networking, children and youth programming, and social events. This one-of-a-kind annual gathering attracts people from all over the world for an uplifting weekend of connection, support, and community.
www.genderodyssey.org

Philadelphia Trans Wellness Conference—Philadelphia, Pennsylvania, USA

This Philadelphia-based conference, as part of the Mazzoni Center's mission, offers education and information for healthcare professionals and the trans community, including friends and family, by addressing a myriad of health and well-being issues, while promoting networking and providing an inclusive environment, which welcomes gender diversity and expression through supporting all voices.
www.mazzonicenter.org/trans-wellness/mazzoni-center-announces-dates-2018-welness-trans-wellness-conference

DOCUMENTARIES/FILMS/MUSIC

Disclosure: Trans Lives on Screen (2020)
1 hour 48 minutes (documentary). Directed by Sam Feder, produced by Sam Feder, Amy Scholder, Laverne Cox, Abigail Disney, Lynda Weinman, Charlotte Cook, Laura Gabbert, Matthew Perniciaro, Caroline Libresco, Michael Sherman, and S. Mona Sinha. A documentary that explores transgender representation in media and how this affects the lives of transgender people and culture in America.
https://www.imdb.com/title/tt8637504

Growing Up Coy (2016)
1 hour 26 minutes (documentary). Directed by Eric Juhola, produced by Still Point Pictures, Eric Juhola, Jeremy Stulberg, Randy Stulberg, and Diana Holtzberg.
As the result of six-year-old Coy Mathis, a transgender girl, not being permitted to use the girls' bathroom in her Colorado elementary school, her parents fight for her right to do so. This true story follows the family's journey as they protect the civil rights of their child and combat discrimination through legal means that prove to be victorious.
https://growingupcoy.com

Gun Hill Road (2011)

1 hour 26 minutes (film). Directed by Rashaad Ernesto Green, produced by SimonSays Entertainment, A Small Production Company, and The Princess Grace Foundation.

An ex-con returns home to the Bronx after three years in prison to discover his estranged wife and his child exploring a gender transformation that will put the fragile bonds of their family to the test.

www.imdb.com/title/tt1525838

Ma Vie En Rose/My Life in Pink (French subtitles in Belgium) (1997)

1 hour 28 minutes (film). Directed by Alain Berliner, produced by Carole Scotta and Canal+ Eurimages CNC.

A drama telling the story of Ludovic, a child who is seen by family and community as a boy, but consistently communicates being a girl. The film depicts Ludovic's family struggling to accept this transgressive gender expression.

https://www.imdb.com/title/tt0119590/

The Most Dangerous Year (2018)

90 minutes (documentary). Directed by Vlada Knowlton, produced by Vlada Knowlton, Lulu Gargiulo, and Chadd Knowlton.

In 2016, a group of Washington State families with transgender children banded together with activists and like-minded law-makers and fought tooth and nail against the wave of anti-trans rights legislation that swept the nation and their home state. This is their story.

www.siff.net/festival/the-most-dangerous-year

Trans in America: Texas Strong (2018)

18 minutes (Emmy-winning documentary). Directed by Daresha Kyi, produced by the ACLU & Little By Little Films, with an LGBT-led team.

An intimate portrait of Kimberly and Kai Shappley, a mother who has to confront her religious community while her young transgender daughter navigates life at school, where she's been banned from the girls' school.

www.youtube.com/watch?v=cuIkLNsRtas&t=5s

The Trans & Nonbinary Kids Mix and Practice Your Pronouns

This mix is a curated playlist of original songs by artists all over the gender map, celebrating life and offering trans/nonbinary youth a reflection of their world. The mix was curated by Julie Be of *Ants on a Log*, and includes joyful, danceable songs, poignant ballads, songs with nonbinary pronouns, folk, hip-hop, pop, and more, offering kids of all ages (and adults) something to love, and lots to celebrate.

https://antsonalog.bandcamp.com/album/trans-nonbinary-kids-mix

ORGANIZATIONS

Ackerman Institute's Gender & Family Project

The Gender & Family Project (GFP) empowers youth, families, and communities by providing gender affirmative services, training, and research. GFP, founded in 2010, promotes gender inclusivity as a form of social justice in all the systems involved in the life of the family.

www.ackerman.org/gfp

The Family Acceptance Project® (FAP)

FAP is providing confidential family support services to help ethnically diverse families decrease rejection and increase support for their LGBT children, including those who are questioning their sexual orientation or gender identity. These services are provided free of charge and are available in English, Spanish, and Cantonese. FAP has collaborated with Child and Adolescent Services at San Francisco General Hospital/University of California, San Francisco (UCSF), and with community providers to develop a new family-oriented model of wellness, prevention, and care for LGBT children and adolescents, based on its research. This new family-related approach helps ethnically and religiously diverse families to decrease rejection and increase support to prevent risk and promote their LGBT children's well-being. FAP provides training on its family intervention approach and using its research-based resources to providers, families, and religious leaders across the United States and in other countries. It is currently implementing FAP's family support model in collaboration with several agencies and communities around the country. This includes a partnership to integrate FAP's family approach into services provided by the Ruth Ellis Center in Wayne County, MI.

http://familyproject.sfsu.edu

FORGE

A progressive organization whose mission is to support, educate, and advocate for the rights and lives of transgender individuals and SOFFAs (significant others, friends, family, and allies). It is dedicated to helping move fragmented communities beyond identity politics and forge a movement that embraces and empowers our diverse complexities. It is a national transgender anti-violence organization, founded in 1994. Since 2009, it has been federally funded to provide direct services to transgender, gender non-conforming, and gender non-binary survivors of sexual assault. Since 2011, FORGE has served as the only transgender-focused organization federally funded to provide training and technical assistance to providers around the country who work with transgender survivors of sexual assault, domestic and dating violence, and stalking. Its role as a technical assistance provider has allowed it to directly see the key continuing and emerging challenges many agencies are experiencing in serving sexual assault survivors of all genders.

https://forge-forward.org

Gender Spectrum

This organization offers information and training for families, educators, professionals, and organizations, helping them to create gender-sensitive and inclusive environments for all children and teens.

www.genderspectrum.org

GLSEN (Gay, Lesbian and Straight Education Network)

Championing LGBTQ issues from K–12 education since 1990, this organization works to ensure that LGBTQ students are able to learn and grow in a school environment free from bullying and harassment. It transforms US schools into the safe and affirming environment all youth deserve, for it believes that every student has the right to a safe, supportive, and LGBTQ-inclusive K–12 education. As a national network of educators, students, and local GLSEN chapters working to make this right a reality, its research and experience have shown that there are four major ways that schools can cultivate a safe and supportive environment for all of their students, regardless of sexual orientation and gender identity or expression.

www.glsen.org

Human Rights Campaign

The Human Rights Campaign (HRC) represents a force of more than three million members and supporters nationwide. As the largest national lesbian, gay, bisexual, transgender, and queer civil rights organization, HRC envisions a world where LGBTQ people are ensured of their basic equal rights, and can be open, honest, and safe at home, at work, and in the community. HRC Foundation's Welcoming Schools is the nation's premier professional development program providing training and resources to elementary school educators on a range of issues, including how to support transgender and non-binary students. HRC's Transgender Children and Youth page includes resources for families, community members, school officials, and more. Co-published with the American Academy of Pediatrics and the American College of Osteopathic Pediatricians, HRC Foundation's *Supporting & Caring for Transgender Children* is a groundbreaking resource that explains how families and healthcare professionals can help transgender and gender-expansive children thrive.

www.hrc.org

www.hrc.org/resources/topic/parenting

www.hrc.org/resources/resources-for-people-with-transgender-family-members

The Jim Collins Foundation

This foundation, in memory of Jim Collins, offers financial assistance towards gender-affirming surgeries.

https://jimcollinsfoundation.org

Lambda Legal
This national LGBT organization offers legal services, impact litigation, education, and public policy work.
www.lambdalegal.org

LGBTQ+ Centers
There are locations, often within large cities, which house LGBTQ+ centers, in the United States and countries worldwide. These centers can sponsor community events, meetings, and workshops for the Transgender Community. Occasionally, some of these meetings or workshops may even host support groups, which focus on the unique needs and challenges that parents and families face. If these centers do not yet have meetings or workshops geared toward supporting parents and families, they are often open to welcoming these programs. This can be viewed as an opportunity to create a series for parents and families by individuals who are knowledgeable of how transitioning affects parents and families, based on the needs of parents and families, and then forming a network or support program. You can search the internet for LGBTQ+ centers in your area.
https://en.wikipedia.org/wiki/List_of_LGBT_community_centers_in_the_United_States

Movement Advancement Project (MAP)
This project offers family support through resources for families of transgender and gender-diverse children. Many people don't understand what it means to be transgender or gender diverse, so some parents or family members struggle when their child comes out as transgender or gender diverse. It is natural for parents to have questions, and this document, jointly created by the Biden Foundation, Gender Spectrum, and the Movement Advancement Project, highlights resources geared toward answering those questions. These resources also help parents gain deeper understanding and learn how to best support their child in ways that can help them succeed and thrive. Parents and family members will learn why family rejection is so devastating and find practical steps for advancing acceptance.
www.advancingacceptance.org
www.lgbtmap.org/advancing-acceptance-for-parents

National Center for Transgender Equality
This organization was founded in 2003 by transgender activists who recognized the urgent need for policy change to advance transgender equality. With a committed board of directors, a volunteer staff of one, and donated office space, it set out to accomplish what no one had yet done: provide a powerful transgender advocacy presence in Washington, DC. Today, it is a team of hard-working staff members supported by a nationwide community of transgender people, allies, and advocates with an extensive record of winning life-saving change for transgender people.
https://transequality.org

National Collegiate Athletic Association (NCAA) Office of Inclusion
As a core value, the NCAA believes in and is committed to diversity, inclusion, and gender equity among its student-athletes, coaches, and administrators. It seeks to establish and maintain an inclusive culture that fosters equitable participation for student-athletes, and career opportunities for coaches and administrators from diverse backgrounds. Diversity and inclusion improve the learning environment for all student-athletes, and enhance excellence within the Association.
www.ncaa.org/about/resources/inclusion/lgbtq-resources
www.ncaa.org/sites/default/files/Transgender_Handbook_2011_Final.pdf

Parents and Friends of Lesbians and Gays (PFLAG)
This is a national non-profit organization with thousands of members and supporters and more than 400 chapters across the United States. This vast grassroots network is cultivated, resourced, and serviced by the PFLAG National Office, located in Washington, DC, the national Board of Directors, and 13 Regional Directors. The organization promotes the health and well-being of gay, lesbian, bisexual, and transgender people, their families, and friends through support, education, and advocacy. An extended family of the LGBTQ+ community, PFLAG families, friends, and allies work together with those who are lesbian, gay, bisexual, transgender, and queer+ to provide opportunities for dialogue about sexual orientation and gender identity. It acts to create a society that is healthy and respectful of human diversity. PFLAG has local chapters across the United States, including groups specifically for families with transgender children.
https://pflag.org/transgender
www.pflaghoco.org

The Trans Youth Equality Foundation
This foundation provides education, advocacy, and support for transgender and gender non-conforming children and youth and their families. It shares information about the unique needs of this community, partnering with families, educators, and service providers to help foster a healthy, caring, and safe environment for all transgender children. In addition, this organization offers programs that include camps, retreats, support groups, and a popular Tumblr blog for youth.
www.transyouthequality.org

Welcoming Schools
Creating safe and welcoming schools for all children and families, HRC Foundation's Welcoming Schools is the nation's premier professional development program providing training and resources to elementary school educators to embrace all families, create LGBTQ and gender inclusive schools, prevent bias-based bullying, and support transgender and non-binary students.
https://www.welcomingschools.org

World Professional Association for Transgender Health (WPATH)

This is a non-profit, interdisciplinary professional and educational organization devoted to transgender health. Members engage in clinical and academic research to develop evidence-based medicine and strive to promote a high quality of care for transsexual, transgender, and gender non-conforming individuals internationally. The Standards of Care information is available on the WPATH website. In addition, this site also offers an opportunity to search for medical and mental health providers who are members of the association.

www.wpath.org

PROFESSIONAL BOOKS

Diane Ehrensaft, PhD (2016) *The Gender Creative Child: Pathways for Nurturing and Supporting Children Who Live Outside Gender Boxes* (Experiment).

In this up-to-date, comprehensive resource, Dr. Ehrensaft explains the interconnected effects of biology, nurture, and culture to explore why gender can be *fluid*, rather than binary. As an advocate for the gender-affirmative model and with the expertise she has gained over three decades of pioneering work with children and families, she encourages caregivers to listen to each child, learn their particular needs, and support their quest for a true gender self.

Laura Erickson-Schroth, MD, MA (ed.) (2014) *Trans Bodies, Trans Selves: A Resource for the Transgender Community* (Oxford University Press).

This encyclopedic resource guide, written by professionals and community members who share their stories and expertise, houses major topics and current information that address the lives of those who are transgender or questioning individuals and others who are affected by these issues.

Elisabeth Kübler-Ross, MD and David Kessler (2005) *On Grief and Grieving: Finding the Meaning of Grief Through the Five Stages of Loss* (Scribner).

Elisabeth Kübler-Ross's last book, written in collaboration with David Kessler, concludes her journey exploring the famous five stages of grief and loss. The authors discuss a vast multitude of issues affecting the varied processes of mourning and grieving.

S.J. Langer, LCSWR, (2019) *Theorizing Transgender Identity for Clinical Practice: A New Model for Understanding Gender* (Jessica Kingsley Publishers).

Providing new approaches for exploring gender identity and expression, this book is ideal for clinical practice with transgender and gender nonconforming/diverse clients. Importantly, it moves beyond the medical model to advance an understanding of transgender subjectivity as a natural variation of gender in humans.

*Lambda Literary Award Finalist – 2020

Arlene I. Lev, LCSW-R, CASAC and Andrew R. Gottlieb, PhD, LCSW (eds) (2019) *Families in Transition: Parenting Gender Diverse Children, Adolescents, and Young Adults* **(Harrington Park Press).**
This is a collection of clinically oriented articles, research, and case material authored by mental health and medical experts, both nationally and internationally known, as well as first-person narratives written by parents and families, exploring the complexities faced by parents and caretakers attending to the needs of their children in a largely hostile world. The professional articles are positioned side by side with the voices of the parents themselves—each complementing the other—together adding up to a richly complex, original tapestry. This text is designed for mental health professionals—clinicians, educators, and researchers; medical providers; parents and caretakers of gender-diverse children, adolescents, and young adults—and is suitable for graduate and doctoral level coursework in a range of subject areas, including gender, sexuality, and family studies.

Elijah C. Nealy, PhD, MDiv, LCSW (2017) *Transgender Children and Youth: Cultivating Pride and Joy with Families in Transition* **(W.W. Norton & Company).**
Therapist and former deputy executive director of New York City's LGBT Community Center, and himself a trans man, wrote this, the first-ever comprehensive guide to understanding, supporting, and welcoming trans kids. This book is full of best practices to support trans kids, covering everything from family life to school and mental health issues, as well as the medical, physical, social, and emotional aspects of transition.

Encian Pastel, Katie Steele, MBA, Julie Nicholson, PhD, Cyndi Maurer, PhD, Julia Hennock, MA, AMFT, Jonathan Julian, MA, AMFT, Tess Unger, MA, and Nathanael Flynn, MA (2019) *Supporting Gender Diversity in Early Childhood Classrooms: A Practical Guide* **(Jessica Kingsley Publishers).**
By offering practical steps for adults who work with young children to build inclusive and intentional spaces where all children receive positive messages about their unique gender selves, this book increases awareness about gender diversity in learning environments such as childcare centers, family child care homes, and preschools. The book is based on some of the most progressive, modern understandings of gender and intersectionality, as well as research on child development, gender health, trauma-informed practices, and the science of adult learning. By including the voices and lived experiences of gender-expansive children, transgender adults, early childhood educators, and parents and family members of trans and gender-expansive children, it contextualizes what it means to rethink early learning programs with a commitment to gender justice and gender equality for all children.

Kryss Shane, MS, MSW, LSW, LMSW. Foreword by PostSecret. Afterword by James Lecesne (2020) *The Educator's Guide to LGBT+ Inclusion: A Practical Resource for K-12 Teachers, Administrators, and School Support Staff* **(Jessica Kingsley Publishers).**
The rates of bullying, truancy due to lack of safety in schools, and subsequent suicidality

for LGBT+ youth are exponentially higher than for non-LGBT+ youth. As a result, many American K–12 students are suffering needlessly and many school leaders are unsure of what to do. This book solves that problem. Setting out best practices and professional guidance for creating LGBT+ inclusive learning in schools, this approachable and easy-to-follow book guides teachers, educators, administrators, and school staff toward appropriate and proven ways to create safer learning environments, update school policies, enhance curricula, and better support LGBT+ youth as they learn. Featuring real-life situations and scenarios, a glossary, and further resources, this book enables professionals in a variety of school roles to integrate foundational concepts into their everyday interactions with students, families, and staff to create an overall school culture that nurtures a welcoming, inclusive, and affirming environment for all. This book can be utilized by independent readers, department teams, and entire school district reading experiences.

Rylan Jay Testa, PhD, Deborah Coolhart, PhD, LMFT, and Jayme Peta, MA, MS (2015) *The Gender Quest Workbook: A Guide for Teens and Young Adults Exploring Gender Identity* (Instant Help).

The activities in this comprehensive workbook will help transgender and gender non-conforming teens explore their identity internally, interpersonally, and culturally. And along the way, TGNC teens will learn how to effectively express themselves and make informed decisions on how to navigate their gender with family, friends, classmates, and co-workers. The book also includes chapters on sex and dating, balancing multiple identities, and how to deal with stressful challenges when they arise. It incorporates skills, exercises, and activities from evidence-based therapies—such as cognitive behavioral therapy—to help TGNC teens address the broad range of struggles they may encounter related to gender identity, including anxiety, isolation, fear, and even depression.

VIDEOS AND WEBSITES

You will find endless videos and websites on the internet that can be incredible resources. It is important to know that each video is usually one person's journey or experience which may or may not help you in your time of need or confusion.

Dear Parents of Trans Youth (2016) Sam Collins
Q&A video to help parents of trans kids. It is candid interview answers to questions based on the experiences of a mom and her trans child.
www.youtube.com/watch?v=gIgs3YrQGaU

Dear Transphobic Parents (2018) ThatEmoKidAlex
Though the title may deter some parents to view this video, the message is important and relevant.
www.youtube.com/watch?v=X8a3-qHWcbE

Gender Dysphoria Affirmative Working Group
A discussion space for medical and mental health professionals, academics, researchers, activists, and allies supporting transgender and gender non-conforming youth.
www.gdaworkinggroup.com

Gender-Inclusive Biology
Teaching biology creates many opportunities to authentically incorporate student curiosity. The Next-Generation Science Standards (NGSS) expect students to ask questions about natural phenomena and then explain their answers using models.
This website offers examples of adapting curriculum to NGSS and gender-inclusive standards, as well as resources for advocating to administration and others.
https://www.genderinclusivebiology.com/ourteam

HealthyTrans
This website suggests some questions that can be asked at medical appointments, which pertain to transgender issues.
www.healthytrans.com

Parents and Transgender Children Read Powerful Affirmations (2017) Iris
Parents are asked to read affirmations to their transgender children.
www.youtube.com/watch?v=t9h7jWYJa5w

To the Parents of Trans Kids (2016) From buzzfeed LGBT on Facebook
This video discusses positive ways transgender kids were and can be supported.
www.youtube.com/watch?v=LVdB2TjneEk

Trans America Videos for Parents of Trans Kids
This is an excellent way to find resources using the key words: trans, America, and kids.
www.youtube.com/results?search_query=trans+America+parents+of+trans+kids

Transgender: A Mother's Story (2017) Susie Green, TEDxTruro
Susie Green shares the inspirational story of her transgender daughter, who told her when she was four that she should have been born a girl. Susie is the CEO of Mermaids, a charity that supports gender-variant children, young people, and their families. Susie became involved with Mermaids when she needed support for her daughter, Jackie. Susie has expanded the charity's capacity and funding, as well as developing the services it offers. She campaigns for the provision of more services and respectful media representation of transgender people. This talk was given at a TEDx event using the TED conference format but independently organized by a local community.
www.youtube.com/watch?v=2ZiVPh12RQY

Transgender Children Talk About Being Raised by Their Families (2017)
Transgender children and their families discuss challenges of growing up in today's world. Transgender children talk about being raised by their families.
www.youtube.com/watch?v=ZLNdExzuKwc

Transgender Kids Are Just Kids After All (2016) Amber Briggle, TEDxTWU
A self-identified feminist mom tells her story of coming to recognize her son for who he is rather than who she assumed he was based on his sex assigned at birth. Gender non-conformity is something often championed by feminists, but trans identity is something else entirely. Amber Briggle is a small business owner, a community volunteer, a political junkie, and the mother of two incredible children—Lulu (age three) and MG (age eight)—who have brought many surprises along the way, including MG's revelation at the age of two that he was mislabeled at birth and identified not as a girl, but as a boy. Through trial by fire, Amber has quickly and earnestly become an advocate for transgender rights, helping her son navigate the world of boy/girl while simultaneously challenging society's gender stereotypes. She is also a board member of the League of Women Voters of Texas, a proud member of Rotary International, and she has a rescue dog named Bluebell who still hasn't figured out how to fetch Amber a glass of wine, but they're working on it. This talk was given at a TEDx event using the TED conference format but independently organized by a local community.
www.youtube.com/watch?v=t_gCASi58Ps

Transgender Myths (2016) Kovu Kingsrod
Kovu Kingsrod discusses myths in relation to transgender voices.
www.youtube.com/watch?v=sduSt9LqFS8&list=PLHHj7HICtRLNiZ8hifS6ApPHBUy-obLpH1

TransGenderPartners.com: Resources for Significant Others,
Friends, Family and Allies of Transgender People
This website offers resources for significant others, friends, family, and allies of transgender people.
www.transgenderpartners.com/resource-for-partners-2

ANECDOTAL AFFIRMATION

ANECDOTAL AFFIRMATION

Being seen
And respected
For who you are
Is the greatest
Gift of all!

This Anecdotal Affirmation is meant to inspire, provoke thought, and empower your learning in any way that opens your heart. Its presence is intended to set the tone and intention of the chapter. This affirmation may be used as a springboard for writing or as a conversation starter with someone else. Ample space has been provided for you to reflect on the Anecdotal Affirmation.

EMPATHY-EMBRACING EXERCISE

Movies and theater have always been a source of information that can both educate and entertain. As the world is beginning to learn about the Transgender community, movie, theater, and television studios are starting to incorporate transgender characters and storylines that address the needs and realities that affect the lives of transgender students, including their life at school. Although teachers, support staff, and administrators are not necessarily the focus of these plots or scripts, some movies, theater, and television shows can enlighten those in the dark. In time, the hope is that the needs and realities of TGNB students will be portrayed in a way that brings both respect and an understanding of what their daily lives look like at school, throughout their transition.

As teachers, support staff, and administrators become aware of transgender issues, the more often they notice their relevance or lack of presence in the world around them. As you begin to observe places where transgender topics are discussed or absent, you may want to document these realities and share your experiences with others. It is important for TGNB students to have their journey and voice recognized in the arts, media, literature, and in everyday situations. Should you find materials that honor the experiences of TGNB students, as well as those who serve them in school settings, it is helpful to share it with others. It is benefical to express if the portrayal of the experiences of TGNB students and all school personnel working with these students appears accurate and realistic. When it does not, state it, and when it does, applaud it! This will be key in educating others!

Can you think of any TV show or series, movie, play, musical, book, or internet resource that has focused on the transition through the point of view of students who identify as transgender, non-binary, and/or are questioning their gender? In addition, can you think of any TV show or series, movie, play, musical, book, or internet resource that has focused on the stories and experiences of those in school settings who serve students who identify as transgender, non-binary, and/or are questioning their gender?

. . . .

. . . .

. . . .

. . . .

. . . .

. . . .

. . . .

. . . .

DESERVING DE-STRESSING DELIGHT

Volunteering

Helping others can be a very humbling experience and may allow you to see the gifts you already possess. Some educators and support staff can reach a point when they wonder if it is acceptable to focus on something else while they are navigating the challenges of their own professional and personal lives. Volunteering can help you understand and observe the various ways others cope with the unexpected, adversity, or things that are out of their control, as well as embrace and celebrate all that life has to offer!

These experiences can teach educators and support staff life lessons that few other circumstances can provide. Many organizations and activist groups regularly seek volunteers. Some require weekly commitments and training or a specific set of skills. If this is too much of a commitment for you at this point in your life, then there are other options.

Being of service to another person, outside your home and workplace, does not always have to be a structured form of volunteering. Maybe a single parent in your area needs a free babysitter for one evening or a neighbor who uses a wheelchair wants help changing a ceiling lightbulb. Perhaps taking the time to simply volunteer to drive a recently widowed relative to a family function or offer your companionship by joining them for a movie matinee could feel quite rewarding.

Volunteering, formally or not, may not only aid another person, but might also show and teach you things about yourself. Doing so can prove to be invaluable at a time when you may feel stressed or unsure of your own thoughts. Maybe working with a particular organization or person will open doors or possibilities to you that you never even considered before you volunteered. Perhaps volunteering will shed a little light on your daily life and assist you in viewing your specific uncertainties and gifts from a different perspective. You may never know until you try!

Journal your reaction to this Deserving De-Stressing Delight.

ANECDOTAL AFFIRMATION

ANECDOTAL AFFIRMATION

You smile,
Now we smile,
You feel complete,
Now we feel
Complete!

This Anecdotal Affirmation is meant to inspire, provoke thought, and empower your learning in any way that opens your heart. Its presence is intended to set the tone and intention of the chapter. This affirmation may be used as a springboard for writing or as a conversation starter with someone else. Ample space has been provided for you to reflect on the Anecdotal Affirmation.

ANSWER KEYS

Matching Pre-Test Answer Keys for Chapters 2–7

Answer Key for Matching Pre-Test 1: C D J G A K H E L B I F

VOCABULARY NUMBER	DEFINITION LETTER	VOCABULARY NUMBER	DEFINITION LETTER
1	C	7	H
2	D	8	E
3	J	9	L
4	G	10	B
5	A	11	I
6	K	12	F

Answer Key for Matching Pre-Test 2: K C D I J G E L B H F A

VOCABULARY NUMBER	DEFINITION LETTER	VOCABULARY NUMBER	DEFINITION LETTER
1	K	7	E
2	C	8	L
3	D	9	B
4	I	10	H
5	J	11	F
6	G	12	A

Answer Key for Matching Pre-Test 3: F D E G C H A L B K J I

VOCABULARY NUMBER	DEFINITION LETTER	VOCABULARY NUMBER	DEFINITION LETTER
1	F	7	A
2	D	8	L
3	E	9	B
4	G	10	K
5	C	11	J
6	H	12	I

Answer Key for Matching Pre-Test 4: K H D I B G E F C J L A

VOCABULARY NUMBER	DEFINITION LETTER	VOCABULARY NUMBER	DEFINITION LETTER
1	K	7	E
2	H	8	F
3	D	9	C
4	I	10	J
5	B	11	L
6	G	12	A

Answer Key for Matching Pre-Test 5: A L G J B C F D E I K H

VOCABULARY NUMBER	DEFINITION LETTER	VOCABULARY NUMBER	DEFINITION LETTER
1	A	7	F
2	L	8	D
3	G	9	E
4	J	10	I
5	B	11	K
6	C	12	H

Answer Key for Matching Pre-Test 6: B F A G K C I D J L H E

VOCABULARY NUMBER	DEFINITION LETTER	VOCABULARY NUMBER	DEFINITION LETTER
1	B	7	I
2	F	8	D
3	A	9	J
4	G	10	L
5	K	11	H
6	C	12	E

Answer Key for Untangle-n-Spell from Chapter 7

1. intersectionality

2. compersion

3. families

4. gender diverse

5. GSA

6. transgender

7. gender identity

8. bottom surgery

9. MTM

10. questioning

11. tracheal shave

12. trans-identified

13. parents

14. gender dysphoria

15. FTF

Answer Key for Word Search

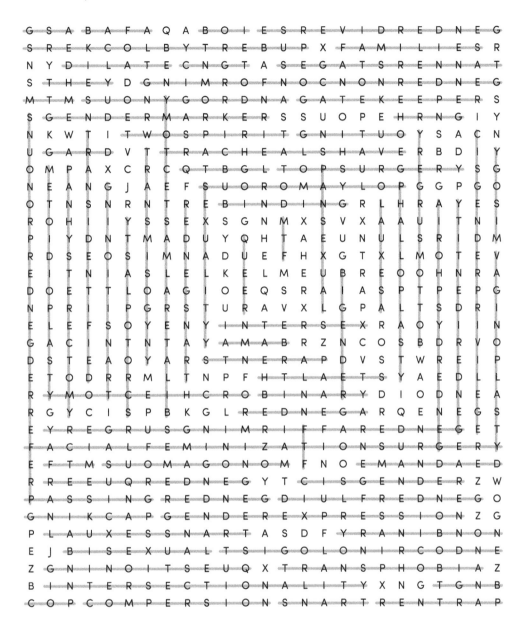

AFAB	dilate	gender	pan hysterectomy	TGNB
agender	drag	non-conforming	pansexual	TGNC
AMAB	endocrinologist	genderqueer	partner	they
androgynous	facial feminization	GnRH	passing	top surgery
asexual	surgery	GSA	phalloplasty	tracheal shave
bigender	FTM/MTM	intersectionality	POC	transgender/
bilateral mastectomy	gatekeeper	intersex	polyamorous	trans-identified
binary	gender	LGBTQ	preferred gender	transitioning
binding	gender-affirming	metoidioplasty	pronouns	transmisogyny
bisexual	surgery	misogyny	puberty blockers	transphobia
boi	gender diverse	monogamous	queer	transsexual
bottom surgery	gender dysphoria	MTF/FTF	questioning	two-spirit
cisgender	gender expression	non-binary	scrotoplasty	vaginoplasty
cisgender privilege	gender fluid	orchiectomy	sexuality	**Bonus Words:**
compersion	gender identity	outing	stealth	families
deadname	gender marker	packing	Tanner stages	parents
				trans

Answer Key for Crossword Puzzle

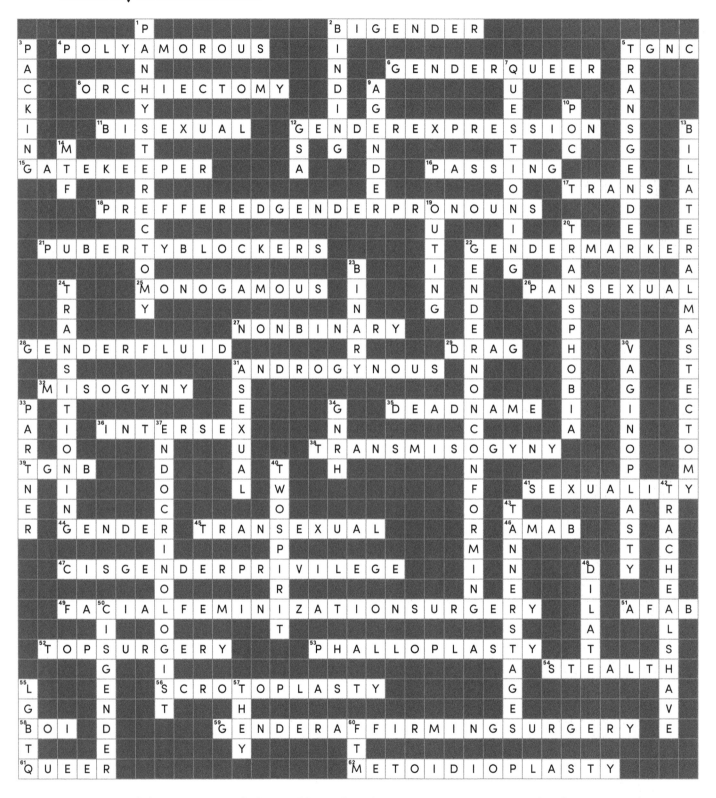

Missing words/terms from vocabulary and bonus lists: bottom surgery, compersion, families, FTF, gender diverse, gender dysphoria, gender identity, GSA, intersectionality, MTM, parents, questioning, tracheal shave, trans-identified, and transgender.

Answer Key for Crossword with Clues

ACROSS

2 BIGENDER: An 8-letter word that means someone who experiences themselves as both masculine and feminine.

4 POLYAMOROUS: An 11-letter word that means a type of relationship where a person is sexually and/or romantically involved with more than one person at the same time.

5 TGNC: A 4-letter abbreviation that stands for Transgender and Gender Non-Conforming, also described as Transgender/Gender Non-Conforming.

6 GENDERQUEER: An 11-letter word that means a gender that is not exclusively masculine or exclusively feminine and is outside the gender binary.

8 ORCHIECTOMY: An 11-letter word that means a type of bottom surgery that involves the removal of testicles.

11 BISEXUAL: An 8-letter word that means a person who is attracted to both masculine and feminine people.

12 GENDER EXPRESSION: A 16-letter term that means the manner in which a person demonstrates their masculinity and/or femininity that can include clothing, body, behavior, speech, gestures, and other forms of appearance.

15 GATEKEEPER: A 10-letter word that means a mental health or medical professional who controls access to medical treatment such as hormones and surgery.

16 PASSING: A 7-letter word that means the ability for a person to be read as their affirmed gender by those who are unaware that the individual's identity is transgender.

17 TRANS: A 5-letter word that means an inclusive umbrella term for all those who identify on the transgender spectrum.

18 PREFERRED GENDER PRONOUNS: A 23-letter term that means the practice of using or referring to a person in the way an individual needs to be addressed, also known as proper gender pronouns.

21 PUBERTY BLOCKERS: A 15-letter term that means a medicine that blocks the hormone GnRH (Gonadotropin Releasing Hormone).

22 GENDER MARKER: A 12-letter term that means the legal designation of one's gender on official documentation or records.

25 MONOGAMOUS: A 10-letter word that means a type of relationship where a person is sexually and/or romantically involved with only one person at a time.

26 PANSEXUAL: A 9-letter word that means someone who is attracted to people of various genders.

27 NON-BINARY: A 9-letter word that means a gender that is not exclusively male or exclusively female and is outside the gender binary.

28 GENDER FLUID: An 11-letter term that means a gender identity and expression that encompasses a variety of aspects related to femininity and masculinity that could change over time.

29 DRAG: A 4-letter word that means enacting gender for the purpose of performance or show.

31 ANDROGYNOUS: An 11-letter word that means someone who possesses both masculine and feminine characteristics.

32 MISOGYNY: An 8-letter word that means a disdain, hatred, or mistrust of all people female and feminine.

35 DEADNAME: An 8-letter word that means a term that describes the name assigned to a person at birth, which they no longer use, for it does not align with their affirmed gender and can also be referred to as their old name.

36 INTERSEX: An 8-letter word that means a group of medical conditions where someone can be born with ambiguous genitalia and/or internal sex organs or chromosomal differences that are not clearly male or female.

38 TRANSMISOGYNY: A 13-letter word coined by Julia Serano to describe a form of misogyny that is focused towards trans women.

39 TGNB: A 4-letter abbreviation that stands for Transgender and Non-Binary or Transgender and Gender Non-Binary, also described as Transgender/Non-Binary.

41 SEXUALITY: A 9-letter word that means the pattern of thoughts, feelings, and arousal that determine sexual preferences.

44 GENDER: A 6-letter word that means how a person internally experiences themselves as male, female, masculine, feminine, some combination of these, or none of them; aspects of these can be culturally defined.

45 TRANSSEXUAL: An 11-letter word that means a person who identifies within the gender binary (either male or female) and may have medical procedures to bring their body in line with their identity. However, not all people who have medical transitions identify as this word.

46 AMAB: A 4-letter abbreviation that stands for an individual who was assigned male at birth by a medical doctor based on the visible appearance of their genitalia at birth.

47 CISGENDER PRIVILEGE: An 18-letter term that means the advantages granted by society to people whose gender aligns with the gender assigned at birth.

49 FACIAL FEMINIZATION SURGERY: A 25-letter term that means a variety of plastic surgery procedures to create a more feminine appearance to the features of the face.

51 AFAB: A 4-letter abbreviation that stands for an individual who was assigned female at birth by a medical doctor based on the visible appearance of their genitalia at birth.

52 TOP SURGERY: A 10-letter term that means a surgical procedure made to create a masculine-appearing chest or to have breast implants.

53 PHALLOPLASTY: A 12-letter word that means a type of bottom surgery that entails the construction of a penis and can include the construction of testicles and the implant of an erection device.

54 STEALTH: A 7-letter word that is used for a transgender person who chooses to keep their trans status private.

56 SCROTOPLASTY: A 12-letter word that means a surgical procedure that creates a scrotal sac and can include testicular implants.

58 BOI: A 3-letter word that can designate a number of sexual orientations and possibilities that are not mutually exclusive and may also refer to someone assigned female at birth but who does not identify as, or only partially identifies as, a girl or woman; moreover, they often identify as lesbians, dykes, or queer.

59 GENDER-AFFIRMING SURGERY: A 22-letter term that means surgery that brings the individual's body into alignment with their gender identity.

61 QUEER: A 5-letter word that refers to a sexual orientation that is not heterosexual and/or anything that is non-heteronormative.

62 METOIDIOPLASTY: A 14-letter word that means a gender-affirming bottom surgery which releases the micro phallus and can include urethra lengthening.

DOWN

1 PAN HYSTERECTOMY: A 15-letter term that means a type of bottom surgery that usually includes removing the uterus, ovaries, and fallopian tubes and which could involve the removal of the cervix.

2 BINDING: A 7-letter word that means a practice of using material or clothing to constrict the breasts that enables a person to flatten their chest.

3 PACKING: A 7-letter word that means the use of prosthetics and/or other materials to enable an individual to possess the appearance and feeling of having a penis and testicles.

5 TRANSGENDER: An 11-letter overarching word which can be used for people whose gender expression and/or gender identity does not align with their sex assigned at birth.

7 QUESTIONING: An 11-letter word that means the act of a person who is attempting to figure out their own sexuality and/or gender.

9 AGENDER: A 7-letter word that means someone who does not identify with any gender.

10 POC: A 3-letter abbreviation that stands for a Person/People of Color.

12 GSA: A 3-letter abbreviation that stands for Gender and Sexualities Alliance, Gay-Straight Alliance, or Gender and Sexuality Alliance and is a school club for students to meet, organize, and educate around issues pertaining to gender and sexuality.

13 BILATERAL MASTECTOMY: A 19-letter term that means a surgical procedure that removes breast tissue from both sides of the chest and can include the construction of a male-appearing chest.

14 MTF: A 3-letter abbreviation that means a person who now identifies as female gendered but was assigned a male gender at birth.

19 OUTING: A 6-letter word that means the act of disclosing someone's sexuality and/or gender identity without their knowledge and/or permission.

20 TRANSPHOBIA: An 11-letter word that means prejudice, fear, disdain, or discrimination in respect of gender non-conforming and transgender people.

22 GENDER NON-CONFORMING: A 19-letter term that means people who do not meet common gender norms.

23 BINARY: A 6-letter word that means the belief that there are only two genders: male and female.

24 TRANSITIONING: A 13-letter word that means the social and/or medical actions a person takes to explore and/or affirm their gender identity.

30 VAGINOPLASTY: A 12-letter word that means the surgical construction of a vagina.

31 ASEXUAL: A 7-letter word that means someone who does not feel sexual attraction to other people.

33 PARTNER: A 7-letter word that means a person who is in a sexual and/or romantic relationship with someone.

34 GNRH: A 4-letter abbreviation which stands for Gonadotropin Releasing Hormone and means a medical term for the hormone that is released by the hypothalamus governing the production of LH (Luteinizing Hormone) and FSH (Follicle-Stimulating Hormone) by the pituitary gland, which causes the gonads to produce estrogen and testosterone.

37 ENDOCRINOLOGIST: A 15-letter word that means a medical doctor who specializes in glands and hormones.

40 TWO-SPIRIT: A 9-letter word that means an Indigenous North American identity embraced by some individuals who incorporate a variety of gender roles, identities, and expressions by embodying both masculine and feminine spirits and traits.

42 TRACHEAL SHAVE: A 13-letter term that means a surgical procedure that reduces the thyroid cartilage, which makes up the Adam's apple.

43 TANNER STAGES: A 12-letter term that means a system to classify the development of puberty in children.

48 DILATE: A 6-letter word that means a prescribed routine post-vaginoplasty where a person inserts medical equipment into the neovagina in order to maintain the creation of the vaginal canal.

50 CISGENDER: A 9-letter word that means someone whose gender assigned at birth and gender identity are aligned.

55 LGBTQ: A 5-letter abbreviation which stands for lesbian, gay, bisexual, transgender, queer, and/or questioning.

57 THEY: A 4-letter word that may also be used as a gender-neutral pronoun to describe a single individual.

60 FTM: A 3-letter abbreviation that means a person who now identifies as male gendered but was assigned a female gender at birth.

GLOSSARY

AFAB An abbreviation that stands for an individual who was assigned female at birth by a medical doctor based on the visible appearance of their genitalia at birth.

agender Someone who does not identify with any gender.

AMAB An abbreviation that stands for an individual who was assigned male at birth by a medical doctor based on the visible appearance of their genitalia at birth.

androgynous Someone who possesses both masculine and feminine characteristics.

asexual Someone who does not feel sexual attraction to other people.

bigender Someone who experiences themselves as both masculine and feminine.

bilateral mastectomy A surgical procedure that removes breast tissue from both sides of the chest and can include the construction of a male-appearing chest.

binary The belief that there are only two genders: male and female.

binding A practice of using material or clothing to constrict the breasts that enables a person to flatten their chest.

bisexual (bi) A person who is attracted to both masculine and feminine people.

boi It can designate a number of sexual orientations and possibilities that are not mutually exclusive and may also refer to someone assigned female at birth but who does not identify as, or only partially identifies as, a girl or woman; moreover, they often identify as lesbians, dykes, or queer.

bottom surgery A surgical procedure that permanently changes the genitals or internal reproductive organs.

cisgender (cis) Someone whose gender assigned at birth and gender identity are aligned.

cisgender privilege The advantages granted by society to people whose gender aligns with the gender assigned at birth.

compersion A feeling of enjoyment while knowing your partner is experiencing joy, usually when they are romantically or sexually involved with another person. Often used as a contrast to jealousy.

deadname A term that describes the name assigned to a person at birth, which they no longer use, for it does not align with their affirmed gender and can also be referred to as their old name.

dilate A prescribed routine post-vaginoplasty where a person inserts medical equipment into the neovagina in order to maintain the creation of the vaginal canal.

drag Enacting gender for the purpose of performance or show.

endocrinologist A medical doctor who specializes in glands and hormones.

facial feminization surgery A variety of plastic surgery procedures to create a more feminine appearance to the features of the face.

FTM (female-to-male)/F2M/MTM An abbreviation that describes a person who now identifies as male gendered but was assigned a female gender at birth.

gatekeeper A mental health or medical professional who controls access to medical treatment such as hormones and surgery.

gender How a person internally experiences themselves as male, female, masculine, feminine, some combination of these, or none of them; aspects of these can be culturally defined.

gender-affirming surgery (GAS) Surgery that brings the individual's body into alignment with their gender identity.

gender diverse A term that recognizes individuals whose gender may not be viewed by others and/or themselves as aligning with cultural norms based on their gender expression, identity, and/or role in society.

gender dysphoria The uncomfortable, distressing, anxiety-provoking, and/or sometimes depressing feelings that occur in people when aspects of their body and behavior are not congruent with their gender identity.

gender expression The manner in which a person demonstrates their masculinity and/or femininity that can include clothing, body, behavior, speech, gestures, and other forms of appearance.

gender fluid A gender identity and expression that encompasses a variety of aspects related to femininity and masculinity that could change over time.

gender identity One's internal sense of being masculine-identified, feminine-identified, neither, or both.

gender marker The legal designation of one's gender on official documentation or records.

gender non-conforming A term for people who do not meet common gender norms.

genderqueer A gender that is not exclusively masculine or exclusively feminine and is outside the gender binary.

GnRH (Gonadotropin Releasing Hormone) A medical term for the hormone that is released by the hypothalamus governing the production of LH (Luteinizing Hormone) and FSH (Follicle-Stimulating Hormone) by the pituitary gland, which causes the gonads to produce estrogen and testosterone.

GSA An abbreviation that stands for Gender and Sexualities Alliance, Gay-Straight Alliance, or Gender and Sexuality Alliance and is a school club for students to meet, organize, and educate around issues pertaining to gender and sexuality.

intersectionality The lens through which one should look at all the multiple identities involved in their or others' lived experience.

intersex A group of medical conditions where someone can be born with ambiguous genitalia and/or internal sex organs or chromosomal differences that are not clearly male or female.

LGBTQQIA+ An all-encompassing abbreviation which stands for lesbian, gay, bisexual, transgender, queer, questioning, intersex, allies, plus others.

metoidioplasty A gender-affirming bottom surgery which releases the micro phallus and can include urethra lengthening.

misogyny A disdain, hatred, or mistrust of all people female and feminine.

monogamous A type of relationship where a person is sexually and/or romantically involved with only one person at a time.

MTF (male-to-female)/M2F/FTF An abbreviation that describes a person who now identifies as female gendered but was assigned a male gender at birth.

non-binary A gender that is not exclusively male or exclusively female and is outside the gender binary.

orchiectomy A type of bottom surgery that involves the removal of testicles.

outing The act of disclosing someone's sexuality and/or gender identity without their knowledge and/or permission.

packing The use of prosthetics and/or other materials to enable an individual to possess the appearance and feeling of having a penis and testicles.

pan hysterectomy A type of bottom surgery that usually includes removing the uterus, ovaries, and fallopian tubes and which could involve the removal of the cervix.

pansexual Someone who is attracted to people of various genders.

partner A person who is in a sexual and/or romantic relationship with someone.

passing The ability for a person to be read as their affirmed gender by those who are unaware that the individual's identity is transgender.

phalloplasty A type of bottom surgery that entails the construction of a penis and can include the construction of testicles and the implant of an erection device.

POC An abbreviation that stands for a Person/People of Color.

polyamorous A type of relationship where a person is sexually and/or romantically involved with more than one person at the same time.

preferred gender pronouns (PGP) The practice of using or referring to a person in the way an individual needs to be addressed, also known as proper gender pronouns.

puberty blockers A term for a medicine that blocks the hormone GnRH (Gonadotropin Releasing Hormone).

queer A word that refers to a sexual orientation that is not heterosexual and/or anything that is non-heteronormative.

questioning The act of a person who is attempting to figure out their own sexuality and/ or gender.

scrotoplasty A surgical procedure that creates a scrotal sac and can include testicular implants.

sexuality The pattern of thoughts, feelings, and arousal that determine sexual preferences.

stealth A word used for a transgender person who chooses to keep their trans status private.

Tanner stages A system to classify the development of puberty in children.

TGNB An abbreviation that stands for Transgender and Non-Binary or Transgender and Gender Non-Binary, also described as Transgender/Non-Binary.

TGNC An abbreviation that stands for Transgender and Gender Non-Conforming, also described as Transgender/Gender Non-Conforming.

they A word that may also be used as a gender-neutral pronoun to describe a single individual.

top surgery A surgical procedure made to create a masculine-appearing chest or to have breast implants.

tracheal shave A surgical procedure that reduces the thyroid cartilage, which makes up the Adam's apple.

trans An inclusive umbrella word for all those who identify on the transgender spectrum.

transgender/trans-identified An overarching word which can be used for people whose gender expression and/or gender identity does not align with their sex assigned at birth.

transitioning The social and/or medical actions a person takes to explore and/or affirm their gender identity.

transmisogyny A word coined by Julia Serano to describe a form of misogyny that is focused towards trans women.

transphobia Prejudice, fear, disdain, or discrimination in respect to gender non-conforming and transgender people.

transsexual A person who identifies within the gender binary (either male or female) and may have medical procedures to bring their body in line with their identity. However, not all people who have medical transitions identify as transsexual.

two-spirit An Indigenous North American identity embraced by some individuals who incorporate a variety of gender roles, identities, and expressions by embodying both masculine and feminine spirits and traits.

vaginoplasty The surgical construction of a vagina.